FOREWARD

Thank you for purchasing Home & Garden Party's very first cookbook. We are blessed to have so many talented Designers as part of th Home & Garden Party family. All of our Designers who participated are excited for you to try their recipes.

Take time to glance through the cookbook, and you will find tasty appetizers, yummy breakfast foods, fresh breads, creative salads, hearty entrees and vegetables and scrumptious desserts. All of the recipes may be prepared in our exclusive Home & Garden Party stoneware or bakeware products.

I know that you will have a good time sharing these recipes with your family and friends. Everyone at Home & Garden Party appreciates your support and wishes you, "Bon Appetit!"

Enjoy,
Penny Carlile
President

Table of Contents

APPETIZERS

BREAKFAST

SALADS & DRESSINGS

VEGETABLES & SOUPS

ENTREES

CAKES

PIES

MISCELLANOUS DESSERTS

SWEET BREADS

COOKIES

CANDY

Appetizers

Pepperoni Pizza Dip

Submitted by Carolyn Yonchuk, PA

(1) 8 oz. pkg. CREAM CHEESE	1/2 cup PIZZA SAUCE
1/2 cup SOUR CREAM	1/2 cup chopped PEPPERONI
1 tsp. dried OREGANO	1/4 cup sliced SCALLIONS
1/8 tsp. GARLIC POWDER	1/4 cup chopped GREEN PEPPER
1/8 tsp. crushed RED PEPPER	1/2 cup shredded MOZZARELLA

Beat cream cheese, sour cream, oregano, garlic powder, red pepper. Spread this into bottom of bakeware or stoneware pie plate. Spread pizza sauce on top and sprinkle with pepperoni, green pepper, and scallions. Bake for 10 minutes at 350 degrees. Remove from oven and top with cheese. Bake 5 minutes more. Serve hot with bread sticks, toasted French bread, or crackers.

Hot Taco Dip

(to use with 9x13" baker)

Submitted by Dana McIntyre, NY

Preheat oven to 350 degrees.
Layer the following ingredients:
1 8 oz. pkg. cream cheese
1 10 oz. can Hormel Chili (no beans)
1 4.5 oz. can green chiles
1/3 to 1/2 can taco sauce (mild, medium, or hot can be used)
1 8 oz. pkg. mixed, shredded taco cheese

Bake at 350 for 20 minutes and serve warm with tortilla chips!

Pumpkin Bread

Submitted by Helen Holthaus, OH

5 EGGS
1 1/4 cup OIL
1 can solid pack PUMPKIN
2 cups all-purpose FLOUR
2 cups SUGAR
2 pkg. VANILLA PUDDING MIX (not instant)
1 teaspoon BAKING SODA
1 teaspoon CINNAMON
1/2 teaspoon SALT

In a mixing bowl, beat the eggs, add oil and pumpkin, beat until smooth. Combine the dry ingredients and gradually add them to the pumpkin mixture. Bake in Home & Garden Party Loaf Pan, (makes 2 loaves) at 325 degrees for 75-80 minutes.

Corn Cheese Dip

Submitted by Helen Holthaus, OH

1/2 cup SOUR CREAM
1/2 cup MAYONNAISE
1/3 cup PICANTE SAUCE
1/4 teaspoon PEPPER
1/8 teaspoon PEPPER
1/8 teaspoon GARLIC POWDER
3 cups shredded CHEDDAR CHEESE
1 12 oz. can WHOLE KERNEL CORN, drained
1/4 cup seeded and chopped JALAPENO PEPPERS

Mix all ingredients together, cover and chill for 2 hours.
Great to serve in Home & Garden small casserole. Goes well with tortilla chips or crackers.

Fancy Cheese Log

Submitted by Sheila Tellez, AZ

2 8 oz. pkgs. CREAM CHEESE (softened)
1 tbs. bottled STEAK SAUCE
1/2 tsp. CURRY POWDER
1 1/2 cup minced, cooked CHICKEN
1/3 cup minced CELERY
1/4 cup chopped PARSLEY
1/4 cup chopped toasted ALMONDS
RITZ CRACKERS

Beat together first 3 ingredients. Blend in nexct 2 ingredients and 2 tbs. parsley. Refrigerate remaining parsley. Shape mixture into a 9-inch log. Wrap in plastic wrap and chill 4 hours, or overnight. Toss together remaining parsley and almonds - use to coat log. Serve with Ritz Crackers. Makes about 3 cups spread.

Shrimp Dip

Submitted by Sheila Tellez, AZ

1 can frozen cream of SHRIMP SOUP (thawed)
8 oz. CREAM CHEESE
1 tsp. LEMON JUICE
dash of GARLIC POWDER
dash of PAPRIKA
1/4 cup OLIVES (finely chopped)

Mix all ingredients together. Blend well. Refrigerate 30 minutes to 1 hour before serving.

Fresh Fruit Dip

Submitted by Sheila Tellez, AZ

1 7 oz. jar MARSHALLMELLOW CREAM
1 8 oz. pkg. CREAM CHEESE
*Optional - 1 can MANDARIN ORANGES

Blend together well. Serve as a delicious dip for all varieties of fresh fruit.

Porcupines

Submitted by Mary Lee Carson, FL

1/2 cup uncooked RICE
1 and 1/2 lb. GROUND BEEF
1/2 cup chopped ONION
1/2 cups GREEN PEPPER, chopped
1 EGG beaten
1 tsp. SALT
2 cans TOMATO SOUP
2 soup cans WATER

Mix all ingredients except soup and water. Make balls at least 2 inches in diameter. Place in our Home & Garden Party 13x9 baker dish. Pour soup and water over balls, cover and bake in 350 degree oven for 1 1/2 hours. Makes 6 servings.

Easy Sausage Balls

Submitted by Treva Castleberry, TN

Ingredients:
2 cups BISQUICK
1 lb SAUSAGE (room temp so your hands don't hurt from the mixing)
1 jar of CHEEZ WHIZ or approx. one cup of shredded cheddar cheese

Mix all together, very well with hands. Scoop out with a cookie scoop and place on an ungreased sheet. Bake at 350 - 375 until golden brown and no longer pink, usually about 20 minutes.

Cocktail Meatballs

Submitted by Karen Davidson, KY

12 ounces lean GROUND BEEF
1/2 cup OATMEAL
1/4 cup chopped ONION
1 EGG
1/4 teaspoon SALT
1/4 teaspoon PEPPER
1 med. size CHILI SAUCE
1 small jar GRAPE JELLY

Preheat the oven to 350 degrees. To prepare the meatballs, in a large bowl, mix the beef, oatmeal, onion, salt, pepper and egg. Roll mixture in small to medium size balls. Place in BEAN POT and place in oven for 30 min.
Add chili sauce and grape jelly. Bake another 30 minutes or until meatballs are done. Serve in BEAN POT.

Monkey Bread

Submitted by Tonia Oda, OH

4 cans buttermilk biscuits
2 1/2 tsp. cinnamon
3/4 cup margarine or butter

1 1/4 cups sugar
1/2 cup brown sugar

Cut biscuits into 1/4's. Place biscuits in a bag with 3/4 cup sugar and 1 tsp. cinnamon and shake to coat well. Arrange pieces in greased Home & Garden Party mixing bowl and set aside.

Bring remaining ingredients to boil in a saucepan. Pour syrup over biscuits.

Bake at 350 degrees for 45 minutes. Turn bread onto a Home & Garden Party 13" platter or a Chip & Dip plate immediately. Eat while warm.

Confetti Bites

Submitted by Kathleen Jones, AZ

2 (8oz.) cans refrigerated CRESCENT DINNER ROLLS
2 (8oz.) pkgs. CREAM CHEESE
3 tbs. salad dressing
1/2 tsp. basil leaves
1/4 tsp. garlic powder
2-3 cups chopped fresh vegetables
McCormick/Schilling Salad Supreme Seasoning

Press roll dough into rectangle baking stone to form crust.

Bake at 350 degrees for 12-15 minutes: cool thoroughly. Combine cream cheese, salad dressing, basil & garlic powder; spread thinly over crust. Top w/vegetables. Sprinkle generously w/seasoning. Cut into squares. Hint: Use bright colored veggies to acquire the "confetti" look.

Hot Ham And Cheese Dip

Submitted by Melinda Fowler, MI

2 pkg.s. 8 oz. CREAM CHEESE
4 cups SHREDDED MILD CHEDDAR CHEESE
1 small ONION diced small
2 small pkgs. HAM; cut in small pieces

Mix all ingredients together in a bowl; then spread into chip dish. Sprinkle additional shredded cheddar cheese on top if desired. Bake at 350 degrees for approximately 20 minutes or until cheese has melted. Great with tortilla chips or crackers.

Melinda's Famous Bean Dip

Submitted by Melinda Fowler, MI

1 can REFRIED BEANS
1 8 oz. SOUR CREAM
1 8 oz. pkg. CREAM CHEESE
4 cups SHREDDED CHEDDAR CHEESE
3 lbs GROUND BEEF
1 small ONION diced
1 small jar medium SALSA

Cook ground beef and onion until meat is done; add refried beans, cream cheese and mix with ground beef. Mix remaining ingredients together. Transfer to chip dish and spread out. Sprinkle top with more shredded cheese. Bake at 350 degrees until mixture is hot and bubbly. Approximately 25-30 minutes. Great served with tortilla chips.

Cheesy Bacon Bites

Submitted by Cindy Pettit, VA

1 package (3 ounces) CREAM CHEESE, soften
1/4 cup real BACON pieces
2 tablespoons chopped ONION
1/8 teaspoon ground BLACK PEPPER
1 package (8 ounces) refrigerated CRESCENT ROLLS

Preheat oven at 350° degrees. Combine the cream cheese, bacon pieces, onion and pepper in our mixing bowl. Separate crescent rolls into two rectangles. Pinch seams together, spread cream cheese mixture on each rectangle. Roll up, starting at the longest side, and then seal, cut each roll into 16 slices. Place slices cut side down, on our round baking stone. Bake for 15 minutes or until brown. Serve warm. Makes 32 appetizers.

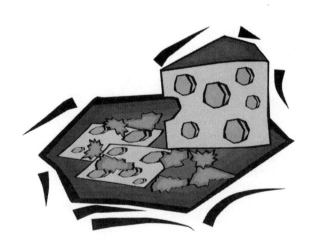

Cheese Bread Sticks

Submitted by Elaine Whitaker, TN

2 1/2 cups All Purpose FLOUR	1 teaspoon SALT
1 teaspoon SUGAR	1 tablespoon QUICK RISE YEAST
1 cup warm WATER (120°-130°)	1 tablespoon OIL

Combine flour, salt, sugar and yeast.

Combine water and oil.

Mix the above combinations to form a soft ball.

Turn onto lightly floured surface and knead 1-2 minutes until smooth and elastic. Place in a lightly oiled bowl turning to coat all sides. Cover and let rise in warm place about 20 minutes

Tip: Place a microwave proof cup of water in your microwave for about 5-8 minutes, remove water. Place the bowl of dough in microwave. This provides a warm place to rise. Punch down risen dough and place on Round Baking Stone. Press out to edges of seasoned or lightly oiled stone using lightly oiled fingers then add topping.

Tip: Seasoning Home and Garden Party's Round Baking Stone: Use paper towel or pastry brush to lightly spread cooking oil on stone. Please don't use a spray such as Pam, this makes your stone tacky feeling.

Topping

1/4 to 1/3 cup ITALIAN DRESSING	1/4 teaspoon SALT
dash of PEPPER	1/4 teaspoon OREGANO
1/4 teaspoon THYME	

Mix well and paint prepared dough crust with mix using pastry brush. Sprinkle with 1 tablespoon grated Parmesan cheese and 1/2 cup Mozzarella cheese.

Bake at 450 degrees on seasoned 14 1/2" Round Baking Stone.

Tip: Please use the Baking Stone Cradle for ease in placing stone in and out of oven. This helps to prevent bums due to difficulty of using just the stone in oven and you won't smash the edge of your breadsticks.

Tip: Double the recipe for thick crust breadsticks or pizza.

Tip: With a few minor changes this is also a great recipe for pizza crust!

Replace Topping with Pizza Sauce and add whatever your imagination wants! ENJOY!!!!

Cheddar Biscuits

Submitted by Shelly Petrey, KY

2 cups of JIFFY or BISQUICK MIX
2/3 cups MILK
1 cup CHEDDAR CHEESE

Mix ingredients together. Spoon onto Home and Garden Party's 14 1/2" round baking stone. Bake at 400° for 10-12 minutes. Meanwhile melt 1/2 stick of butter and add 1/2 teaspoon of garlic salt. Brush butter mixture on hot biscuits. This is a wonderful addition to any meal. Yields 8-10

"Gourmet" Round Bread

Submitted by Evelyn (Katie) Jackson, IN

Step 1.   Go to the store.
Step 2.   Go to the frozen food department
Step 3.   Get yourself a bag of frozen bread dough.
Step 4.   Take it home.
Step 5.   Take one loaf out and wrap it in plastic wrap in the bottom of your fridge.
Step 6.   The next day, take thawed dough out of fridge.
Step 7.   Oil the flower pot of your choice (I like the floral).
Step 8.   Make the loaf into a ball and place in the flour pot.
Step 9.   Cover with plastic wrap that has been oiled or sprayed with cooking spray.
Step 10.   Let rise until a little over the top of the pot.
Step 11.   Read the bag on how to set the oven.
Step 12.   Bake like the bag says except it may take longer. Just cook it till it is golden brown and thuds when you tap the top. (Thud is in the ear of the hearer.)

(continued)

Step 13.   Take it out of the oven. It is real pretty.
Step 14.   Cool it.
Step 15.   Wash the pot.
Step 16.   Wrap the bread in that pretty plastic wrap and put it back in the flower pot.
Step 17.   Wrap the flower pot in clear plastic and put a bow on it.
Step 18.   Give it to a friend.
Step 19.   Call your Home and Garden Party Designer and buy a new flower pot.
Step 20.   Repeat from Step 1.

Cheesy Pizza Dip

Submitted by Glenda Brown, MD
(FOR 9" PIE PLATE)

2 pkg. (8 oz.) CREAM CHEESE softened
2 teaspoons dried ITALIAN SEASONING
2 cups shredded MOZZARELLA CHEESE
1 1/2 cups shredded PARMESAN CHEESE (not grated- shredded)
12 ounces SALSA (you determine how hot!)

Preheat oven to 350°. Combine cream cheese and Italian seasoning; spread into bottom of pie plate. In small bowl, combine cheeses, sprinkle half over cream cheese mixture. Spread salsa over the cheese mixture, then sprinkle remaining cheese over the salsa. Bake 18-20 minutes or until bubbly. Serve with chips or vegetables.

Vidalia Onion-Cheese Dip

Submitted by Karen Fields, KY

3 large VIDALIA ONIONS, coarsely chopped
2 tablespoons MARGARINE or UNSALTED BUTTER, melted
2 cups (8 ounces) shredded sharp CHEDDAR CHEESE
1 cup MAYONNAISE
1/2 teaspoon HOT SAUCE
1 clove GARLIC, minced

Cook onion in butter in a large skillet over medium-high heat, stirring constantly, until tender.
Combine onion, cheese, mayonnaise, hot sauce, and garlic, stir well. Pour into your design of choice casserole dish.
Bake, uncovered, at 375 degrees for 20 to 25 minutes or until bubbly and golden. Serve in your matching chip and dip set with tortilla chips or assorted crackers Yield 4 cups.

Mexican Nacho Dip

Submitted by Nancy Propst, PA

1 (15 oz.) can CHILI without beans
1 jar of your favorite SALSA
1 (8 oz.) pkg. CREAM CHEESE, softened
1 (12 oz.) shredded CHEDDAR CHEESE

Mix the chili, cream cheese, salsa and 3/4 of the shredded cheese. Blend thoroughly and transfer to the "Pie Plate". Top with the remaining shredded cheese. Microwave til hot and cheese is melted. Serve with taco chips, ENJOY!

Fruit Dip

Submitted by Mary Alice Green, ID

1 tub STRAWBERRY CREAM CHEESE
1 large MARSHMALLOW CREAM

Stir well and serve with fresh fruit on Chip & Dip.

Shrimp Chip Or Cracker Dip

Submitted by RuAnn Yearsley, ID

1 qt. COTTAGE CHEESE
1 pint SOUR CREAM
1 8 oz. CREAM CHEESE
2 cans SHRIMP, drained
1 bunch GREEN ONION
SALT
PEPPER

Blend with mixer. Serve on Chip & Dip. Better if mixed up night before.

Reuben Dip

Submitted by Sherrill Funk, OH

16 oz. SAUERKRAUT
16 oz. shredded MOZZARELLA
16 oz. shredded CHEDDAR
16 oz. CARL BUDDIG CORNED BEEF (cubed)
1 cup MAYO
small can of sliced BLACK OLIVES (optional)
cocktail size RYE BREAD

Mix all ingredients (except bread) in mixing bowl and transfer to casserole dish. Bake uncovered for 45-60 minutes or until cheese is bubbly.
Serve hot and spoon dip onto cocktail Rye bread.
This recipe can be halved for a smaller portion.

Caramel Fruit Dip

Submitted by Shelley Herrmann, OH

GREAT SERVED IN CHEESE CROCK

1 pkg. CREAM CHEESE
1/2 cup CARAMEL ICE CREAM TOPPING
1/4 cup HONEY
1/4 tsp. CINNAMON

Beat cream cheese until smooth. Beat in rest of ingredients.
Chill and serve with sliced fruits or graham crackers. Enjoy!

Kielbasa Bites

Submitted by Ronda Hart, MI

2-3 lbs (packages) Kielbasa
Brown Sugar

Cut Kielbasa into 1/4 inch slices. Place Kielbasa in Bean Pot and sprinkle with brown sugar every layer or so, and generously on top.
Bake in oven at 350° for an hour or so (will brown nicely) and serve hot.

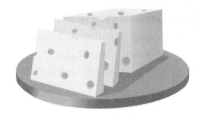

Cheesy, Cheesy Dip

Submitted by Judy Gunter, VA

1 lb. SAUSAGE
1 lb. GROUND CHUCK
2 lb. VELVETTA CHEESE
1 12 -18 oz. jar of SALSA (mild or hot)
1 can CREAM MUSHROOM SOUP

Fry and scramble the sausage and ground chuck together. Pour any drippings off of meat. Cut cheese into blocks and melt in meat mixture. Add soup and salsa and blend together well . Pour into H & G P bean pot or flower pot. Fill Chip n Dip platter with tortilla chips, corn chips and serve!!! Watch it disappear quickly!!!
****Heat the bean pot or flower pot.

Chili Dip

Submitted by Sandy Brandt, WI

1 package of CREAM CHEESE
1 15 oz. HORMEL CHILI WITH NO BEANS
1 16 oz. mild SALSA
1 cup CHEDDAR CHEESE
1 cup MOZZARELLA CHEESE

Cut up fresh tomatoes, black olives, onions, green peppers and hot peppers. Heat oven to 350°. Spread cream cheese on bottom of the stoneware baker or pie plate. Take the chili and half of the salsa and mix it together then spread on top of cream cheese. Take the rest of the salsa and spread on top the chili. Next layer the cheese and vegetables. Heat in oven till bubbly about one half-hour. Serve with corn chips or bread sticks.

Garden Dip

Submitted by Annette DeMay, OH

1 pint MAYONNAISE
1 pint SOUR CREAM
1 tablespoon ACCENT SEASONING SALT
1 tablespoon GARLIC SALT
1 tablespoon PARSLEY FLAKES
1 tablespoon DILL WEED
1 tablespoon ONION FLAKES

Mix and refrigerate to let spices blend. Serve with fresh veggies of your choice such as baby carrots, red & green peppers, radishes and cucumbers. Arrange veggies on any one of the beautiful Home & Garden Party Hostess 2 party booking gift chip & dip sets. Add dip to the center of the veggies. Serve & enjoy!!!

Hot Broccoli Dip

Submitted by Linda Camp, OH

2 cups fresh BROCCOLI FLORETS, finely chopped
4 tablespoons ONION, chopped
4 tablespoons RED BELL PEPPER, chopped
1 ounce (3/4 cup) PARMESAN CHEESE, grated (Divided)
3 GARLIC CLOVES, pressed
2 cups shredded CHEDDAR CHEESE
1 cup fat free SOUR CREAM
1 cup fat free MAYONNAISE
1 teaspoon ground BLACK PEPPER
CHIPS OR BREAD for dipping

Preheat oven to 375 degrees. Chop broccoli, onion and bell pepper. Add 4 tablespoons Parmesan cheese to mixture. Press garlic and add to vegetable mixture along with all other ingredients, mixing well. Spoon into chip and dip. Bake 20-25 minutes or until heated through. Sprinkle remaining Parmesan cheese over top. Serve hot with chips of bread.

Chili Con Queso

Submitted by Renee Lewis, LA

1 lb. VELVETTA CHEESE, melted
1 (15 oz.) can CHILI WITH BEANS
1 (4 oz.) can GREEN CHILES, chopped
1 medium ONION, finely chopped

Mix all ingredients and bake in Bean Pot for 35 minutes at 350 degrees. Serve with chips.

Necole's Taco Dipping

Submitted by Necole Stutes, OH

2 packages of CREAM CHEESE
2 tablespoons of SOUR CREAM
1 package of TACO SEASONING
1 ONION chopped finely

Mix together in Home and Garden Party Mixing Bowl.
Pour into the Home and Garden Party Make It Bake It Take It Dish (aka Chip and Dip) .
Then layer whatever taco toppings you enjoy, for example: lettuce, tomato, onion, black olives, cheese, salsa (in the little bowl). Serve chilled with nacho chips. Perfect for parties, family reunions, picnics or just as a family dinner.

Cracker Dip

Submitted by Linda White, VA

1 cup MAYONNAISE
1/2 cup SOUR CREAM
1 cup grated SWISS CHEESE
ONION FLAKES to taste to your liking
dash of SALT and PEPPER to taste
1/8-1/4 teas. of SEASON SALT
1 box of your favorite WHEAT CRACKERS

Mix all ingredients together in the Home and Garden Party cereal bowl and serve from it as well. Place cereal bowl on top on a dinner plate with crackers around plate. Or use Home and Garden Party Chip and Dip.

Hot Crab Dip

Submitted by Elaine Carroll, MD

1/2 lb. (8 oz.) MARYLAND CRAB MEAT
1 8 oz. CREAM CHEESE, softened
1/2 cup SOUR CREAM
2 tbsp. MAYONNAISE
1 tbsp. LEMON JUICE
1 1/4 tsp. WORCESTERSHIRE SAUCE
2 tbsp. OLD BAY SEASONING or DRY MUSTARD
1 tbsp. MILK
1/4 cup CHEDDAR CHEESE, grated
1/4 cup chopped ONION

In large bowl mix cream cheese, sour cream, mayonnaise, lemon juice, Worcestershire sauce, Old Bay or mustard until smooth. Add enough milk to make mixture creamy.

Stir in copped onion, 2 tbsp. grated cheese. Fold in crab meat. Pour into greased 1 qt. casserole dish. Top with remaining cheese.

Bake 325° about 40 minutes, until mixture is bubbly and browned on top.

Serve warm with crackers or Rye bread. Makes about 4 cups.

Breakfast

Apple Oven Pancakes

Submitted by Nanci Hunter, MI

1 cup MILK
6 EGGS
2 tablespoons BUTTER, melted
1 teaspoon VANILLA
1 cup FLOUR
1/2 teaspoon SALT
2 packages (12 oz. each) frozen ESCALLOPED APPLES
1 tablespoon POWDERED SUGAR
1 teaspoon CINNAMON

Preheat oven to 450 degrees. Spray either the 13x9 Baker or the chip plate with nonstick cooking spray. In bowl combine milk, eggs, butter and vanilla. Add flour and salt. Beat till smooth. Pour batter into pan and bake for 10 minutes. Reduce heat to 350 degrees and continue to bake another 15 minutes or until sides are crisp and golden brown. Heat apples in microwave according to package directions. Remove pancakes from oven. Fill center with apples. Combine powdered sugar and cinnamon and sprinkle over pancake and apples. Cut into wedges or squares and serve. Serves 4.

South of the Border Quiche

Submitted by Kim Kennebeck, IL

16 oz. shredded COJACK CHEESE
   or 8 oz. Shredded MONTEREY JACK CHEESE
8 oz. COLBY CHEESE
5 EGGS
1/2 tsp. CUMIN
1/4 tsp. WHITE PEPPER
1/2 cup GREEN ONION chopped & sauteed in 1 tablespoon of butter
1 can drained and sliced BLACK OLIVES
1/4 tsp. GARLIC POWDER
1 box PILLSBURY ALREADY PIE CRUST (2 crusts)
OPTIONAL INGREDIENTS: serve with SOUR CREAM & SALSA

Preheat oven to 350 degrees.

Mix first 7 ingredients together adding cheese last.

Flour 1 side of 1 crust and put in the Home & Garden Party 9 in. pie plate.

Add mixed ingredients and top with remaining crust.

Use a fork to press edges together and slice off excess crust from sides. Bake at 350 for 45 minutes to 1 hour. To test for doneness, insert a butter knife into the center, it should come out clean. Top crust should be golden brown. Cool 5-10 minutes to allow cheese to set. Slice and serve with Sour Cream and Salsa.

Brunch Breakfast Pizza Squares

Submitted by Margie Elling, MI

1 pound bulk PORK SAUSAGE
1 tube (8 ounces) refrigerated CRESCENT ROLLS
4 EGGS
2 tablespoons of MILK
1/8 teaspoon PEPPER
3/4 cup shredded CHEDDAR CHEESE

In a skillet, cook sausage until no longer pink. Drain. Unroll crescent rolls into a lightly greased 9x13 baking dish. Press dough 1/2 in up the sides seal seams. Sprinkle sausage over dough. In a bowl, beat eggs, milk and pepper. Pour over sausage. Sprinkle with cheese. Bake uncovered at 400 degrees for 15-20 minutes until crust is golden brown and cheese is melted. Serves 8 but you will want more then one piece.

Ham, Egg, and Cheese Casserole

Submitted by Crystal Dunt, MI

5 cups of BREAD CUBES OR CROUTONS
1 lb. HAM; chopped
2 cups CHEDDAR CHEESE; cubed small
4 cups of MILK
1/4 tsp. PEPPER
6 EGGS
1/3 cups CORN OIL
1 tsp. SALT
1 tsp. DRY MUSTARD
1/3 cup FLOUR

Place cubed cheddar cheese, crouton (or bread) and ham in the bottom of a 9x13 bakeware stone. Mix the remaining ingredients together and pour over the cheese, croutons and ham mixture. Refrigerate overnight. Bake at 300 degrees for 1 1/2 hours the next morning. Let sit for 10-15 minutes before serving. Cut into squares and serve on Home & Garden Party Dinner Plates. Serves 12-15 people.

Park Avenue Stuffed French Toast

Submitted by Kathie Van Loon, MI

(Do Ahead) 9x13 Baker

1 LOAF OF WHITE BREAD (egg bread is great if you can find it)
8 EGGS
1 8 oz. CREAM CHEESE
1 1/2 cups HALF AND HALF
3/4 cup SYRUP (maple type)
6 tbs. melted BUTTER
1 tsp. CINNAMON
1 tsp. VANILLA

Cube bread; layer half in "seasoned" 9x13 baking dish.
Cut cream cheese into 16 squares and scatter over the bread.
Cover with remaining bread cubes.
Mix all remaining ingredients and pour over the bread.
Press bread to soak up mixture.
Cover and refrigerate overnight.
Bake covered (foil) at 350 degrees for 40-50 minutes.
Serve with warm maple syrup.

Judy's Overnight Breakfast Egg Stuff

Submitted by Judy Smith, MI

12 EGGS
1 qt. MILK
1 loaf of day old WHITE BREAD, crust removed
2 packages of beef SMOKY LINK SAUSAGES
4 oz. MILD CHEDDAR CHEESE
4 oz. SHARP CHEDDAR CHEESE

Whisk the eggs until fluffy. Add the milk to the eggs.

Cut the sausages into 1" pieces. Remove the crusts from the bread and break it into bite size pieces. Stir in the bread, sausages and cheeses until moistened. Add more milk if needed.

Pour into the casserole dish, cover and refrigerate overnight. In the morning, bake at 350° for 75 minutes, until it is golden brown and a toothpick test comes out clean. Serves 12 large portions.

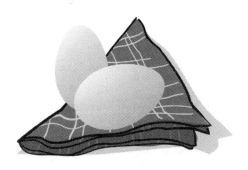

Stuffed French Toast with Strawberry Sauce

Submitted by Leslie Cohen, VA
TO BE USED IN 9X13 BAKEWARE DISH
OR IN CHIP AND DIP DISH

1 loaf FRENCH BREAD, cubed (with crust)
8 ounces CREAM CHEESE, cut into small chunks
12 EGGS
1/4 cup MAPLE SYRUP
1 stick BUTTER, melted

Spread cubed french bread in greased 9x13 bakeware dish or in chip and dip dish. Scatter cream cheese through bread.
In blender, combine remaining ingredients well. Pour egg mixture over bread. (If using the chip and dip dish, place dip dish in center before pouring egg mixture over bread). Cover and refrigerate for at least 1 hour or overnight. Bake at 350 degrees uncovered for 50 to 60 minutes. (remember to allow time in temperature transition to prevent thermal shock). Yields: 10-12 servings.

Strawberry sauce:
2 cups strawberries or 10 ounces frozen strawberries
2 cups strawberry preserves
Combine ingredients in small saucepan and stir constantly until preserves malt and sauce is hot. Serve warm with stuffed french toast. (Pour into dip bowl if using chip and dip dish)

Breakfast Pizza

Submitted by Lesley O'Meara, MI

2 pkgs. CRESCENT ROLLS
2 pkgs. COUNTRY GRAVY MIX prepared, follow pkg. directions
1 roll SAUSAGE (cooked and drained)
2 cups MOZZARELLA CHEESE

Press rolls on bottom and half way up side of 9x13 baker.
Bake as directed on can or until lightly browned.
Prepare gravy and cook sausage. Pour gravy over rolls.
Sprinkle sausage over gravy, then add cheese.
Bake for additional 5-10 minutes
This is great for a brunch.

Chip and Dip Sunday Brunch

Submitted by Leverna L. Garoutte, CA

12 oz. browned, crumbled and drained SPICY SAUSAGE OR BACON
1/2 cup chopped GREEN ONION
9 large EGGS
3/4 cup HALF AND HALF
1 16 oz package frozen SHREDDED HASH BROWN POTATOES, thawed.
2 cups SHREDDED CHEDDAR CHEESE
1 teaspoon SALT
1/2 teaspoon PEPPER

Spray chip and dip platter with cooking spray. Spread potatoes on bottom, followed by bacon or sausage, green onion and cheese. Beat eggs, half and half, salt and pepper together till foamy. Pour over other ingredients. Bake in a preheated 350 degree oven for 60 minutes or until knife comes out clean. You can serve with salsa in the dip bowl if you like. This also works well with the stoneware baking dish.

Breakfast Casserole

Submitted by Raelene Decker, PA

7 slices WHITE BREAD, cubed
1 lb. HAM, BACON, OR SAUSAGE (precooked)
12 oz. SHREDDED CHEDDAR CHEESE
6 EGGS
2 cups MILK
1/2 teaspoon DRY MUSTARD
SALT & PEPPER to taste

TOPPING:
3 tablespoons melted BUTTER
1 1/2 cups crushed CORN FLAKES

Cover the bottom of the Home and Garden Party 9x13 Baker with bread crumbs. Next make a layer of ham, bacon, or sausage over the bread. Top the meat layer with shredded cheese. Set aside.

Whip together eggs, salt, pepper, milk, and dry mustard. Pour over pan ingredients. Cover pan and place in refrigerator overnight. Melt margarine. Crush corn flakes. Mix these together and set aside until morning.

The next morning preheat oven to 350 degrees. Spread topping on casserole. Bake for 45-60 minutes. Remove and let stand 5 minutes before serving.

Breakfast Casserole

Submitted by Marie Pronschinske, WI

2 lbs. LINK SAUSAGE
8 slices of BREAD
3/4 lb. AMERICAN CHEESE
4 EGGS
1 can of CREAM OF MUSHROOM SOUP

Fry, and then drain sausage, cut up the sausage into 1/2 inch pieces. Cut the crust of the bread off. Grate the cheese. Then put the bread, cheese and sausage into the Chip N Dip platter in layers. Then beat the eggs and add milk to the eggs, pour the egg mixture over the bread mixtures. Top with the cream of mushroom soup. Put in refrigerator 1 1/2 hours or overnight. Then take out of the refrigerator and bake at 325 degrees for about 1 1/2 hours. Serve right in the Pottery item. Serves about 8 people.

Pigs In A Blanket

Submitted by Sheila Tellez, AZ

1 pkg. MINI LINK SAUSAGES
3 cans (8 count) CRESCENT ROLLS

Place little sausage at the largest part of tri-shaped crescent roll and roll up to the smallest end. Place the bead side down on an ungreased cookie sheet. Bake at 400 degrees for 10 to 15 minutes until rolls are brown.

Salads & Dressing

Grandma's Macaroni Salad

Submitted by Karen Davidson, KY

1 cup medium size SHELL, CORKSCREW, OR ELBOW MACARONI
1/2 cup cubed CHEDDAR OR AMERICAN CHEESE (2 ounces)
2 lg. GREEN ONIONS WITH TOPS, finely sliced
1/4 cup finely chopped SWEET GREEN, RED, OR YELLOW PEPPER
1/4 cup chopped SWEET PICKLES

For the dressing:
1/4 cup reduced-fat MAYONNAISE
1/4 cup reduced-fat SOUR CREAM
2 tablespoons low-fat MILK
2 tablespoons PICKLE JUICE
2 tablespoons MINCED PARSLEY
1/4 teaspoon each SALT AND BLACK PEPPER

Cook the macaroni according to package directions. Drain well. Rinse with cold water. Drain again.

Meanwhile, in BEAN POT, combine cheese, green onions, green pepper, & sweet pickles. To prepare the dressing, in a small bowl, whisk together mayonnaise, sour cream, milk, pickle juice, parsley, salt and pepper, pour over cheese mixture. Toss lightly to coat. Fold in macaroni. Cover and refrigerate for 4 to 8 hrs. Makes 4 side-dish servings.

Broccoli Bacon Salad

Submitted by Marie Pronschinske, WI

Cut into large bowl:
1 bunch of BROCCOLI (raw) chopped, tops only
1 head of CAULIFLOWER (raw) florets cut into pieces
1 small RED ONION
1 small package of GREEN PEAS (uncooked)
1 lb. BACON fried and drained, cut into pieces and cool.

Optional: sunflower seeds, cucumbers diced, raisins, or
                    oriental noodles crushed
Dressing:
1 cup MAYONNAISE
1/2 cup SUGAR
2 tsp. VINEGAR

Mix dressing ingredients in the batter bowl when blended well pour over the broccoli and cauliflower mixture. Chili - Bean Pot, or mixing bowl, or Chip N Dip, after ingredients are combined. Pour into one of the desired pottery pieces and serve.
ENJOY!!!

Poppy Seed Dressing

Submitted by Sheila Tellez, AZ

1 1/2 cup SUGAR
2 tsp. DRY MUSTARD
2 tsp. SALT
2/3 cup VINEGAR
3 tbs. ONION JUICE
2 cups SALAD OIL (not olive oil)
3 tbs. POPPY SEEDS

Mix sugar, mustard, salt and vinegar - add onion juice and stir thoroughly. Slowly add oil - beating constantly and continue to beat until thick (either use blender or electric mixer).
When you think mixture is thick enough - beat 5 minutes longer - add poppy seeds and beat for a few minutes. Store in a cool place or refrigerate. To "make" onion juice - put onion in electric blender and strain off juice (use medium size onion).

Orange Delight Salad

Submitted by Sheila Tellez, AZ

1 pkg. ORANGE JELLO (dry)
1 9 oz. COOL WHIP
1 small carton COTTAGE CHEESE
1 lg. can CRUSHED PINEAPPLES (drained)
1 can MANDARIN ORANGES (drained)
1 can COCONUT

Combine all ingredients - draining fruit. Refrigerate. Quick-Easy - and Delicious!

Glazed Fruit

Submitted by Sheila Tellez, AZ

BANANAS - 5 to 6
1 can PEACH PIE FILLING
1 can MANDARIN ORANGES (drained)
1 can CRUSHED PINEAPPLE (drained)
1 sm. pkg. sliced FROZEN STRAWBERRIES (thawed)
pecans

Mix together. Easy & Delicious!

Great Fruit Salad

Submitted by Sheila Tellez, AZ

1 can dark CHERRY PIE FILLING
reg. size COOL WHIP
1 can EAGLE BRAND MILK
1 cut COCONUT
large can (drained) CRUSHED PINEAPPLE
1/2 cup PECANS (chopped)
3 to 4 med chopped BANANAS
1 1/2 cup mini MARSHMELLOWS

Mix all together. Easy - Fast - & Delicious!

French Salad Dressing

Submitted by Nancy Propst, PA

1 cup WESSON OIL	1/4 cup CIDER VINEGAR
1/3 cup KETCHUP	1/2 cup SUGAR
1 tsp. PAPRIKA	1 tsp. SALT
2 tsp. LEMON JUICE	1 med. ONION

Toss all ingredients into a blender and blend thoroughly.
Use the "Creamer" to serve.

Yummy HOT Fruit Salad

Submitted by Debbie Lagerhausen, IL

1 medium jar APPLESAUCE
1 small can APRICOTS
1 small can PEACHES
1 small can PEARS
1 small can PINEAPPLE CHUNKS
1 large can CHERRY PIE FILLING
1 teaspoon CINNAMON
1/4 cup BROWN SUGAR

*Do Not Drain Fruits
*In 9x13 Baker, layer with Applesauce first
*then Apricots, Peaches, Pears & Pineapple
*Pour Cherry Pie Filling over Fruits
*Sprinkle Cinnamon & Brown Sugar
*Bake at 350 degrees for 1 hour

**Taste great on Ice Cream or topped w/ Ganola & Whip Cream!
Enjoy!

Cucumber Delight

Submitted by Judy Gunter, VA

4 large (skinny) CUCUMBERS, peeled and thinly sliced
2 ONIONS, slices thin and separated by rings
1 - 1 1/2 cups MAYONNAISE
3 tbsp. MILK
SALT & PEPPER to taste

Chill Flower Pot (99537) for 1 hour before mixing
above ingredients ......

Fold mayonnaise and milk into LARGE MIXING BOWL (99540) with
cucumbers and onions. Continue to stir until all cucumbers and onions
are covered evenly and mixture is Smooth. Salt and pepper to taste
serve in chilled Flower Pot. A great side dish/salad for almost any food.

Annie's Sassy B-B-Q Sauce

Submitted by Annie Allen, KS

2 tablespoons BROWN SUGAR
1 teaspoon CELERY SEED
SALT & PEPPER to taste
dash (or more if your sassy too!)
1 cup KETCHUP
1/4 cup WATER

1 tablespoon CHILI POWDER
1 teaspoon GARLIC SALT
1 teaspoon LIQUID SMOKE
TABASCO SAUCE
1/4 cup APPLE CIDER VINEGAR

Mix above ingredients together thoroughly in a Gravy Boat for thick
pouring or place in dispenser to season meats to taste. Use to season
Chicken, Pork or Beef. Makes 1 1/2 cups. Refrigerate after use.

Shells & Tomato Salad

Submitted by Mary Louise Law, KY

3 cups uncooked LARGE SHELL PASTA
1 can (14.5 oz.) HUNT'S CHOICE CUT DICED TOMATOES, drained
    (sometimes I use herb/garlic tomatoes)
1 can (2 1/4 oz.) sliced RIPE OLIVES, drained
1/4 cup each: SLICED GREEN ONIONS, DICED GREEN BELL
PEPPER, DICED YELLOW BELL PEPPER and thinly sliced CARROTS
1/4 cup ITALIAN DRESSING (I use Italian Tomato & Herb.)
2 tbs. grated PARMESAN CHEESE

Cook pasta to desired doneness. Drain and rinse with cold water to cool. In a Bean Pot combine cooked pasta and all remaining ingredients. Mix well. Sprinkle with cheese. Makes 6 servings. Prep Time: 15 Minutes

Summer Cole Slaw

Submitted by Lynn Elliott, IL

(It's great to take because there is no mayonnaise to go bad)

1 bag of PRE-MIXED COLE SLAW
3 or 4 GREEN ONIONS
1/3 cup of OIL
1/3 cup of CIDER VINEGAR
1/3 cup of SUGAR
1 pkg. of SLIVERED ALMONDS
1/2 cup of SUNFLOWER KERNELS
1 pkg. of beef RAMEN NOODLES

Using the MIXING BOWL, empty the contents of the pre-mixed cole slaw bag into the bowl. Crumble the Ramen noodles over the top of the coleslaw, setting aside the seasoning packet that is enclosed.

Sprinkle the almonds into the BAKEWARE PIE PLATE and toast in the oven for 15 minutes at 225 degrees. Let cool. Add sunflower kernels and cooled almonds to the cole slaw and Ramen noodle mixture. Dice the green onions and add to mixture. Stir until evenly mixed.

Just before serving combine the oil, cider vinegar, sugar and seasoning packet in the HALF GALLON BELLY PITCHER and stir well. Pour over the cole slaw mixture and mix well. Put entire contents into a chilled BEAN POT and serve.

Cauliflower and Broccoli Salad

Submitted by JoAnn Eldridge, MN

4 cups chopped CAULIFLOWER
4 cups chopped BROCCOLI
1 cup chopped GREEN ONION
1 cup MAYONNAISE
1 teaspoon SUGAR
2 teaspoon VINEGAR
1 teaspoon (Beau Monde) SEASONING SALT

Mix and refrigerate (it's better after it sets)

Fruit Cole Slaw

Submitted by Diane Boykas, PA

2 cups CABBAGE, finely shredded
1/4 cup PINEAPPLE TIDBITS
1 ORANGE sectioned
1 APPLE, chopped
3 tbsp. PECANS OR WALNUTS chopped
1/2 cup YOGURT
1/4 cup APPLE OR GRAPE JUICE

Mix cabbage and fruit in the casserole dish. Combine yogurt with juice.
Pour over fruit mixture and mix well. Refrigerate until serving. Keep
covered to keep cold.

Spaghetti Salad

Submitted by Shelley Petrey, KY

Place your Home and Garden Party bean pot, mixing bowl or flower pot in the freezer.
Bring to boil 1 lb. box of angel hair pasta, drain and cool.

Chop following ingredients:

TOMATO

ZUCCHINI

CARROTS

BLACK OLIVES (optional)

GREEN PEPPER

SQUASH

ONION (optional)

Mix together with pasta, add a 16 oz. bottle of Italian Dressing and stir. Pour in cold Home and Garden Party pottery and enjoy.

Cold Broccoli Salad

Submitted by Jennifer Kelly, PA

This recipe can be served in the Bean Pot or Covered Casserole.
Put the Bean Pot in the freezer while you are preparing the
recipe to "seal" in the cold.

2 heads BROCCOLI (cut into small bite size pieces)
2 finely chopped GREEN ONIONS
1 lb. BACON (fried and crumbled)
2 cups CHEDDAR CHEESE (shredded)
Mix above ingredients

Dressing:
1/2 cup SUGAR
1 cup MAYONNAISE
2 tbsp. VINEGAR

Cream above dressing ingredients and pour over the top of the broccoli
mixture. Blend well. Put salad into Bean Pot and let sit in the refrigerator
ahead of time. Great to serve at picnics. The salad remains cold for
hours!

Green Klondike Salad

Submitted by Barb Crespin, OH

2 small boxes LIME JELLO (or 1 large box)
3 cups HOT WATER
8 oz. COOL WHIP
4 KLONDIKES (ice cream bars)

Dissolve jello in hot water. Cool. Place in refrigerator until syrupy. Beat with rotary beater. Mix Cool Whip and chopped-up Klondikes. Add to beaten jello and whip all together. Place (pour) into 13" platter. Chill. Serves 8-9.

Banana Split Salad

Submitted by Ronda Hart, MI

1 can SWEETENED CONDENSED MILK (14 oz.)
1 carton FROZEN WHIPPED TOPPING, thawed (12 oz.)
1 can CHERRY PIE FILLING (21 oz.)
3 medium firm BANANAS, cut into chunks
1 can CRUSHED PINEAPPLE, drained (8 oz.)
1/2 cup CHOPPED NUTS
(I also added 4 or 5 FRESH STRAWBERRIES sliced)

In the bean pot, combine the milk and whipped topping until well blended. Fold in the rest of the ingredients, chill. 10 servings.

Cookie Salad

Submitted by Dana Sandberg, MN

2 - 16 oz. cartons of COOL WHIP
1 - quart of BUTTERMILK
4 - small boxes of FRENCH VANILLA PUDDING
4 - packages of FUDGE STRIPED COOKIES
2 - big cans of MANDRIN ORANGES

Mix the quart of buttermilk with the boxes of pudding in the mixing bowl. Then add the Cool Whip, and Mandrin Oranges. Break the cookies into bite size pieces and ONLY put in the batch right before you serve it. Otherwise they will be soggy.
Then place some of the whole cookies to top for decoration. Enjoy!
Remember to chill your mixing bowl before you serve it.

Creamy Broccoli - Raisin & Peanut Salad

Submitted by Mary Anne Tobin, CT

1 1/2 lbs. FRESH BROCCOLI
1/2 cup RAISINS
1/2 cup DRY ROASTED PEANUTS
2 tablespoons finely chopped ONION
2 slices BACON cooked, crumbled and divided

Wash and remove the ought stalk end of the broccoli. Cut into 1" pieces using the stalk and florettes. Combine broccoli, raisins, peanuts, onion and half of the bacon -toss gently - set aside.

Dressing
6 oz. CREAM CHEESE, softened
4 tablespoons SUGAR
4 tablespoons WHITE VINEGAR
4 tablespoon VEGETABLE OIL
2 tablespoons PREPARED MUSTARD
2 cloves GARLIC, minced

Combine cream cheese, sugar, vinegar, veg. oil, mustard in blender or food processor - process until smooth.

Pour over broccoli mixture. You will have some leftover depending on how much dressing you like. Stir well - chill for 3 hours. Just before serving sprinkle remaining bacon on top. Hope you enjoy!!

I had to be different so this morning - 1 added some chopped fresh cauliflower. I imagine - you could add chopped carrot and other vegetables. It passed the husband test - so it has to be good!!
I put this in my magnolia flower pot and with the color combination it is a really pretty dish. I can not wait to take this to the family picnic this afternoon. Maybe I will even book a few more parties!!!

Bean Pot Veggie Salad

Submitted by Carol Trehey, WI

1 can dark red KIDNEY BEANS (drained)
1 can FRENCH STYLE GREEN BEANS (drained)
2 - 5 oz. boxes of SPIRAL PASTA (rotoni)
1/3 cup chopped GREEN ONIONS
1 can diced CARROTS (drained)
1 small package of fROZEN PEAS
1/2 cup chopped CELERY
1/4 cup chopped GREEN PEPPERS
VINEGAR

Dressing: Mix together well the following ingredients
2 cups MIRACLE WHIP
1 scant cup SUGAR
1 cup WHIPPING CREAM (NOT whipped cream)

Drain can of kidney beans and soak in vinegar for 1 hour then drain off vinegar. Cook, drain, rinse and cool pasta, Mix all ingredients together and place in your Home and Garden Party Bean Pot and put in your refrigerator overnight. For variety you can add shrimp or imitation crab meat cut in bite size chunks.

Vegetables
& Soups

Potato Casserole

Submitted by Crystal Dunt, MI

2 lb. of frozen HASH BROWNS
1/2 cup chopped ONIONS
1 can CREAM OF CHICKEN SOUP
16 oz. of SOUR CREAM
8 oz. shredded CHEDDAR CHEESE
1/2 cup of crushed CORNFLAKES (optional)

Heat oven to 375. Combine all the ingredients (except the cornflakes) and spread into the 9x13 bakeware. Top with cornflakes and bake for 50 minutes to 1 hour until done.

This recipe makes an excellent side dish for any holiday or you can even serve it at breakfast time. This serves up to 10-12 people easily! This recipe you may use the fat free or low fat ingredients as well. Either way it's still delicious!

Chunky Potato Soup

Submitted by Connie Bottoff Ashcroft, NY

3 tbsp. BUTTER
1/4 cup FLOUR
4 cup MILK
2 cup peeled diced POTATOES
1/2 cup chopped ONION
3/4 tsp SALT
1/2 tsp PEPPER

Melt butter in heavy saucepan over low heat. Add flour, stirring until smooth. Simmer-stirring often for 30 minutes or until mixture has thickened and potato is done.

A can of cream corn may be added as well as ham or bacon, mushrooms, clams.

Barbecued Green Beans

Submitted by Kim Ruder, IN

3 cans cut GREEN BEANS, drained
1/2 lb. BACON
1 med. ONION, chopped
1 cup KETCHUP
1 cup BROWN SUGAR

Fry bacon, drain, save grease in skillet. Fry onion till tender. Crumble bacon in bottom of our 9x13 baker. Put onion over that. Put the green beans over the bacon/onion mixture. Combine ketchup and brown sugar and pour over all. Bake 200° for 2 1/2 hours. Great for cookouts!

Potato Casserole

Submitted by Nancy Propst, PA

8-10 medium POTATOES
2 Tbsp. FLOUR
SALT & PEPPER
2 Tbsp. minced fresh PARSLEY
1 (8 oz.) pkg. CREAM
2 Tbsp. minced CHIVES (or 1 small grated onion)
CHEESE, softened
1 (3 1/2 oz.) can FRENCH ONION RINGS, lightly crushed
2 EGGS, beaten lightly

Peel and boil potatoes till tender. Drain and beat until smooth with electric mixer. Add cream cheese, pepper, and beat again. Blend in eggs, flour, parsley, and chives and beat thoroughly. Check the seasoning and pour into a buttered "Flower Pot". Spread crushed onion rings over top and bake, uncovered, at 325° for 30 minutes or until puffy and golden.

Wisconsin Hashbrown Casserole

Submitted by Melissa Weltz, OH

2 lb. Bag COUNTRY STYLE HASHBROWNS
2 sticks MARGARINE
1 pt. SOUR CREAM
1/2 cup chopped ONION
1 can CREAM OF CHICKEN SOUP
2 cups shredded CHEDDAR CHEESE
1 tsp. PEPPER
1 cup CORNFLAKES (crushed)

Preheat oven to 325°. Spread thawed potatoes in 9x13 Home & Garden Party Baker. Pour 1 stick melted margarine over the potatoes. In Home & Garden Party's Mixing Bowl, mix together sour cream, onion, soup, cheese and pepper. Spread mixture over potatoes. Combine 1 stick melted margarine and crushed cornflakes and sprinkle over top. Bake for 1 hour.

Granny's Baked Beans

Submitted by Anette DeMay, OH

2 cups PORK & BEANS (16 oz. can)
1/3 cup bottled BBQ SAUCE
1/4 cup BROWN SUGAR
1/4 cup GOLDEN RAISINS
1/3 cup TART (GRANNY SMITH) APPLE
1/2 cup chopped ONION
8 BACON STRIPS

Drain pork & beans and place in your beautiful Home & Garden Party bean pot. Chop onions & add to beans. Add bbq sauce, brown sugar and raisins. Mix together. Lay bacon strips on top. Bake at 350 for 1 hour.

Garlic Cheese Potatoes

Submitted by Ruthann Martinez, AZ

1/2 stick BUTTER
2-3 cloves of GARLIC, pressed
2 chopped SCALLIONS
1/4 cup grated PARMESAN CHEESE

Place peeled and sliced potatoes in the Bean Pot. Melt butter 1/2 stick butter with 2-3 cloves pressed garlic. Pour over potatoes. Sprinkle 2 chopped scallions over potatoes and 1/4 cup grated Parmesan cheese. Cover with the lid, bake at 400° for 20 minutes, or until done. Remove top and let brown for 7 minutes.

Pork Roast Caribbean Style

Submitted by Nancy Hutter, MT

1 can sliced PINEAPPLE, undrained
2 tablespoons BROWN SUGAR
2 teaspoons ground CUMIN
1 teaspoon CINNAMON
1/2 teaspoon dried THYME
1/8 teaspoon ground RED PEPPER
3 cloves of GARLIC, pressed
1 boneless PORK ROAST (about 4 lbs.)
1 1/2 pounds peeled SWEET POTATOES
2 medium RED ONIONS
1/2 teaspoon SALT
1/2 teaspoon BLACK PEPPER

Drain pineapple and reserve 1/2 cup of the juice for marinade. Combine reserved juice, brown sugar, spices and garlic in a bowl. Place juice and roast in container and refridge overnight or at least 5 hours.

Preheat oven to 350 degrees. Cut potatoes into quarters. Cut onions into wedges and pineapple rings into quarters.

Remove roast from marinade and place into baker pan. Place veggies and pineapple around roast. Sprinkle with salt and pepper, cover and bake 1 hour. Then remove covering and bake 20 to 30 minutes longer or until thermometer reaches 155 degrees. Let stand for 10 minutes before carving. Serves 6.

Screwie Louie Hotdish

Submitted by Chris Gloege, MN

1 pound pkg RAINBOW ROTINI NOODLES, cooked and drained
2 cups cooked and chopped CHICKEN OR TURKEY
1 can CREAM OF MUSHROOM CONDENSED SOUP
1 can CREAM OF CHICKEN CONDENSED SOUP
1 cup MIRACLE WHIP
2 cups shredded PIZZA CHEESE
1 cup frozen VEGGIES (peas/ carrots)

Mix together and put in the Bean Pot and top with one more cup of shredded cheese.
Either bake it now or put it in the fridge overnight. If you chill it, remove it and put it on the counter for about an hour before you bake it. Bake at 350 degrees for 1 hour. This is a great recipe to use with leftover Holiday turkey.

Pizza Pasta

Submitted by Chris Gloege, MN

1 pound package RAINBOW ROTINI NOODLES, cooked, drained
    and rinsed with cold water
3 medium TOMATOES, chopped
1 pound CHEDDAR CHEESE, cubed
1 tablespoon fresh chopped CHIVES
3 oz. sliced or chopped PEPPERONI

Mix together.

In a one cup measuring cup or small bowl combine:
1/4 cup vegetable oil
1 Tablespoon Parmesan cheese
1/4 cup white vinegar
2 tsp. dried Oregano
1 tsp. salt
1 tsp garlic powder
1/4 tsp pepper

Pour over noodle mixture and mix together. Chill it in the mixing bowl.
It has the best flavor if it chills overnight. Toss before serving.

Best Ever Beans
And Sausage

Submitted by Sharon Green, ID

(This is a large recipe and so our 9x13 baker is perfect for it. It won't fit in most other 9x13 pans.)

1-1/2 pounds PORK SAUSAGE
    (Suggestion: Jimmy Dean 12 oz. original and 12 oz. hot)
1 medium GREEN PEPPER, chopped
1 medium ONION, chopped
1 can (31 oz.) PORK AND BEANS, undrained
1 can (15 oz.) GREAT NORTHERN BEANS, undrained
1 can (15 oz.) GARBANZO BEANS, undrained
1 can (15 oz.) RED KIDNEY BEANS, rinsed and drained
1 can (15 oz.) BLACK-EYED PEAS, rinsed and drained
1 can (15 oz.) PINTO BEANS, rinsed and drained
1-1/2 cups KETCHUP
3/4 cup packed BROWN SUGAR
2 tsp. DIJON MUSTARD

In a large skillet, brown sausage; drain. Add green pepper and onion; saute until tender. Drain and pat dry. Add remaining ingredients; mix well. Pour into a lightly greased 9x13 baker. Cover and bake at 325 degrees for 1-1/2 hrs. Uncover and bake 30 minutes longer or until bubbly.

Old Settler Beans

Submitted by Kim Miller, WI

1/2 POUND GROUND BEEF
1/2 cup BROWN SUGAR
1/4 POUND BACON
1/2 cup WHITE SUGAR
1 SMALL ONION
2 Tbsp. MOLASSES
1 (16 oz.) KIDNEY BEANS
1/4 KETCHUP
1 (16 oz. PORK & BEANS
1 tsp. MUSTARD
1 (16 oz.) BUTTER BEANS

Mix all ingredients in Bean Pot and bake at 300 degrees for 3 hours.

Hash Brown Casserole

Submitted by Tina DeVillez, IN

6 medium POTATOES, cleaned, peeled, & shredded
1/2 cup chopped ONION
1/4 cup chopped GREEN PEPPER
1 cup SOUR CREAM
1 cup MILK
1 package shredded CHEDDAR CHEESE

Mix all together in Bean Pot. Cover & bake in 350 degree oven for approximately 1 hour until potatoes are done. Stir after about 30 minutes of baking. May add extra milk if too thick.

Broccoli Cornbread

Submitted by Karen Fields, KY

1 10-ounce package frozen chopped BROCCOLI thawed
1 (8 1/2 ounce) package CORN MUFFIN MIX
4 large EGGS, lightly beaten
3/4 cup small-curd COTTAGE CHEESE
1/2 cup BUTTER or MARGARINE, melted
1/3 cup chopped ONION
1 teaspoon SALT

Drain broccoli well, pressing between layers of paper towels. Combine corn muffin mix and next 5 ingredients; stir well. Stir in broccoli. Pour into 13x9 baker. Bake at 400 degrees for 20 to 25 minutes or until golden.
Let cool slightly, and cut into squares and place on your pattern choice platter.

Grandma Helen's Baked Beans

Submitted by Catherine Alton, CA

1 lb GROUND BEEF or TURKEY
1 pkg ONION SOUP MIX
1/2 cup WATER
1 cup KETCHUP
2 tablespoons MUSTARD
2 teaspoons VINEGAR
2 - 1 lb (12 oz.) cans PORK & BEANS

Brown meat and drain. Mix all ingredients together in the Bean Pot, Bake at 300 degrees for 2 hours. Serves 8-12.

Home And Garden
Sweet Potato Casserole

Submitted by Judy Schaff, NV

1 HOME & GARDEN BEAN POT
1 can (29 oz.) cut SWEET POTATOES-drained
1 can (8 oz.) CRUSHED PINEAPPLE-drained
1/2 cup MAPLE SYRUP
1/2 cup PECAN HALVES
1/4 cup sliced dried APRICOTS
1/4 cup BROWN SUGAR
1 tablespoon BUTTER or MARGARINE-melted
1/4 teaspoon SALT
1 teaspoon GROUND CINNAMON
1 teaspoon PUMPKIN PIE SPICE

Place sweet potatoes in ungreased Bean Pot. Combine remaining ingredients and pour over potatoes. Bake at 350 degrees for 45 minutes. I place a layer of tin foil between lid and top. Can remove and add some miniature marshmallows and brown for the last 5-10 minutes of bake time. DO NOT USE BROILER TO BROWN.

Calico Beans

Submitted by Fay Smith, VA

1 pound HAMBURGER - crumbled and browned, drain grease
1/2 pound BACON - fried crisp and crumbled
1/2 cup chopped ONION
2 teaspoons VINEGAR
1/2 cup KETCHUP
1 teaspoon SALT
1 teaspoon PREPARED MUSTARD
3/4 cup BROWN SUGAR
1 can each - LIMA BEANS, KIDNEY BEANS, PORK & BEANS

Mix all ingredients together and simmer in a crock pot. Serve in a Home & Garden Party Bean Pot.

Potato Casserole

Submitted by Fay Smith, VA

Preheat oven to 375°.
Mix the following ingredients together:
1 - 2 lb. bag of FROZEN HASH BROWN POTATOES
1 - large ONION - chopped
1 - can CREAM OF CELERY SOUP
1/2 pound melted MARGARINE or BUTTER
1 - 16 ounce container SOUR CREAM
SALT AND PEPPER to taste

Spoon mixture into a 9x13 Home & Garden Party Baker. Top with crumbled potato chips. Bake for 45 minutes to 1 hour.

Cheesy Buffet Potatoes

Submitted by Glenda Brown, MD

2 lbs. (or more) FROZEN HASHBROWN POTATOES
   (found Ore Ida Country Hash Browns work best)
8 oz. SOUR CREAM
10 oz. grated CHEDDAR CHEESE
2 cans CREAM OF CHICKEN SOUP
1/4 cup dried CHIVES
1/2 cup MARGARINE, melted

Thaw potatoes. Combine remaining ingredients. Stir in potatoes. Pour into greased 9x13 Baker. Bake for 1 hour at 350. Makes a great "buffet" dish!

Twice Baked Potatoes

Submitted by Emily Allison, VA

2 lb. pkg. frozen loose HASHBROWN POTATOES
1/4 cup MARGARINE, melted
1 cup (8 oz.) SOUR CREAM
1 can CREAM OF CHICKEN SOUP
1 can CREAM OF MUSHROOM SOUP
1 medium ONION, chopped
1 cup grated CHEDDAR CHEESE
2 cups RICE KRISPIES, crushed

Combine all ingredients except Rice Krispies. Coat 9 x 13 bakeware dish with vegetable spray. Pat potato mixture in dish. Sprinkle Rice Krispies on top. Cover with aluminum foil. Bake at 350 degrees for 1 hour.

Tater Tot Casserole

Submitted by Debbie Wolf, PA

8 oz. SOUR CREAM
2 medium ONIONS, chopped
2 cans CREAM OF CHICKEN SOUP
1 cup SHREDDED CHEDDAR CHEESE
Stir these ingredients together in the greased 9x13 baker.

2 lb. bag of TATER TOTS
1 cup shredded CHEDDAR CHEESE
Press tater tots into the above mixture and top with cheese

Bake at 350° for 1 hour and 30 minutes. I don't preheat oven because of putting the frozen tater tots into a hot oven.

I always make this recipe in our 9x13 baker because it tastes better if it sets for about 30 minutes after you take it out of the oven and our baker keeps it warm during that time. (Great for picnics)

Baked Bean Casserole

Submitted by Ronda Hart, MI

2 lb. of KIELBASA
1 large ONION
4 cans of BUSH'S BAKED BEANS
1 cup of KC MASTERPIECE BBQ SAUCE
1 tablespoon of CAJUN SEASONING* (can be bought at GFS)
1 lb. of shredded COLBY JACK CHEESE
2 - 8 oz. CRESCENT QUICK DINNER ROLLS (unbaked)

Cut up Kielbasa into 1" pieces, and cut up onion, then fry them together. Once they are fully cooked, add the Baked Beans, BBQ Sauce, and Cajun Seasonings and cook until it is heated and mixed well. Poor that into our 9x13 Baker and add Crescent Quick Dinner Rolls on top evenly to cover the whole top, then layer cheese and top and cook until rolls are done. (about 15-18 minutes).
*GFS = Gordons Food Service or you can get it from Sam's Club

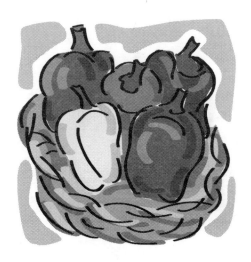

Sweet Potato Casserole

Submitted by Amy Conkey, OH

6 cups (cooked and mashed) SWEET POTATOES
   (canned and drained or fresh) (40 oz. can = 3 cups)
1 cup SUGAR
2 stick of BUTTER, MARGARINE or BUTTER FLAVORED CRISCO
2 tbsp. VANILLA
4 EGGS

Beat all ingredients well and place in margarine coated 9x13 baking dish. (Home & Garden 9x13 Baker)

TOPPING
2 cups BROWN SUGAR
2/3 cup MARGARINE
2 cups of CHOPPED NUTS (Walnuts are very good).

Mix topping ingredients w/fork and sprinkle (or place) over potato mixture. Bake at 350 degrees for 45 minutes to 1 hour.

Quick Corn Chowder

Submitted by Sharon Siebert, IL

1 GARLIC clove, pressed
2 cans (13 1/2-14 1/2 oz. each) ready-to serve CHICKEN BROTH
1 small ONION, chopped
1 can (15 oz.) CREAM-STYLE CORN
1/2 cup RED OR GREEN BELL PEPPER, chopped
1/4 teaspoon BLACK PEPPER
1 tablespoon BUTTER OR MARGARINE
1/2 cup SOUR CREAM
2 medium POTATOES
1 tablespoon PARSLEY

In a bean pot, add the pressed garlic, chopped onion, bell pepper and butter. Microwave on HIGH 1 1/2-2 minutes or until vegetables are crisp tender. Cut potatoes in 1/2 inch cubes. Add potatoes, chicken broth, corn and black pepper. Cover loosely with lid. Microwave on HIGH 25-30 minutes or until potatoes are tender, stirring once halfway through cooking. Stir in sour cream, microwave on HIGH 2-3 minutes or until heated through. Sprinkle with parsley and serve.

Sour Cream Potatoes

Submitted by Bridget Gibbs, VA

2 cups SHARP CHEDDAR CHEESE
1/2 cup finely chopped ONION
6-8 medium POTATOES
16 oz. SOUR CREAM
2 tsp. melted BUTTER OR MARGARINE

Boil potatoes in water until fully cooked. Let cool, then peel skin off potatoes and shred. Mix in Cheddar cheese, onion, sour cream and butter and stir until completely blended. Place in a greased 9x13 baking stone. Bake for approximately 35-45 minutes at 425 degrees.

Rocky Mountain Baked Beans

Submitted by Linda Jenkins-Schneider, OH

(This recipe will make you a star!)
Most important item needed: one Home & Garden Party Bean Pot (your favorite pattern, of course)

Mix following together in large bowl:
2 cans PORK & BEANS (1 lb. 13 oz. size)
2 medium ONIONS - cut into big chunks and separated
2 large GREEN BELL PEPPERS - cut into big chunks
2 teaspoons WORCESTERSHIRE SAUCE
Stir together before adding:
1 cup KETCHUP   **1 cup BROWN SUGAR**

Combine all ingredients and pour into Home & Garden Bean Pot. Bake, covered at 325 degrees for 3 hours, stirring twice. Uncover the last 30 minutes.

Sweet Potato Casserole

Submitted by Gwenda Rotz, PA

1 - 29 oz. can SWEET POTATOES, drain and mashed
1 cup SUGAR
2 EGGS
1/2 cup MILK
1/2 tsp. SALT
1/3 stick BUTTER, melted
1 t. VANILLA
Mix well and pour into butter pie plate

Topping:
1 cup BROWN SUGAR
1/2 cup FLOUR
1/3 cup BUTTER melted
1 cup PECAN crushed

Crumble over top. Bake 350° for 35 minutes uncovered.

Sensational Sweet Baked Beans

Submitted by Ginny Macbeth, ID

1 large can PORK & BEANS
1/2 cup chopped ONION
1 tbsp. chopped GREEN PEPPER
2 tbsp. WORCESTERSHIRE SAUCE
1/2 cup BROWN SUGAR
1/2 cup KETCHUP
1 small can PINEAPPLE CHUNKS
1/4 lb. BACON

Barely brown bacon, onion, and green pepper. Put rest of ingredients in your favorite Home & Garden Party Bean Pot. Add barely browned ingredients. Bake uncovered in a 350 degree oven for 1-2 hours. (A longer time at a slightly lower temperature is OK, too.)

Eggplant Parmesan Casserole

Submitted by Marilyn Borntrager, VA

1 lg. firm EGGPLANT
1 qt. homemade or good quality SPAGHETTI SAUCE W/MEAT
8 oz. grated MOZZARELLA CHEESE
PARMESAN CHEESE
2 EGGS
ITALIAN PARSLEY or BASIL
Large BAKING DISH (9x13x2)

Slice eggplant thin, fry quickly in hot oil (lightly brown). Drain in colander (about 6 hours.) or if you are a weight watcher, arrange eggplant slices on cookie sheet and lightly brown in 350° oven. Set aside.

Cover bottom of casserole dish with enough spaghetti sauce to just cover, a layer of eggplant, sprinkle with grated parmesan cheese, salt and pepper and some shredded mozzarella cheese. Repeat and finish with sauce. Bake at 400° for 20 minutes. Remove from oven.
Beat 2 eggs with 1/2 or 3/4 cup of milk (like scrambled eggs) add salt and pepper, add 1 Tbsp. Italian parsley or basil, 1/4 cup of parmesan cheese and rest of mozzarella cheese. Pour over eggplant. Return to oven and bake at 450° for about 10 minutes or until knife inserted into center of casserole comes out clean. This will be puffy like souffle. Enjoy with salad, garlic bread and red wine.

Corn Pie

Submitted by Diane Boykas, PA

DOUBLE PIE CRUST
2 tbsp. melted BUTTER
1/2 cup MILK
3 tbsp. chopped GREEN OR RED PEPPER
2 tbsp. chopped ONION
2 tsp. SALT

2 EGGS (lightly beaten)
3 tbsp. FLOUR
2 (15 1/4 oz.) cans CORN

2 hard boiled EGGS

Line pie plate with crust. Beat together the 2 eggs, butter, flour and milk. Mix the corn, peppers, onions and salt in a separate bowl. Add the milk mixture to the corn mixture and mix until well blended. Pour into pie shell. Add 2 sliced eggs on top. Cover with the second crust and seal the edges well. Cut several vents in the top.

Bake at 350° for 1 hour until golden. Slice and place in cereal bowl, and pour warm milk over top. Serve warm. (Place in microwave to reheat).

Vegetable Stew

Submitted by Diane Boykas, PA

1 large ONION, chopped
1 large ZUCCHINI, cubed
6 TOMATOES, cut-up (or 1 - 28 oz. can)
2 tbsp. MOLASSES
1 tsp. SALT
1 cup cubed POTATOES

2 cups sliced CARROTS
1 cup PEAS (or 1 - 15 1/4 oz. can)

1 tsp. BASIL
1 tsp. PEPPER

Combine all ingredients in Bean Pot. Cover and cook in 350° oven for 30-45 minutes until vegetables are tender.
Serve in soup bowl, sprinkle with grated mozzarella cheese.

Beef Vegetable Soup

Submitted by Mary Louise Law, KY

1 lb. ground BEEF	1/2 cup chopped ONION

1 package HAMBURGER HELPER MIX FOR BEEF NOODLE

5 cups WATER	1 BAY LEAF
1/4 teaspoon SALT	1/8 teaspoon PEPPER

1 can (16 oz.) WHOLE TOMATOES
1 package (10 oz.) FROZEN MIXED VEGETABLES or
    2 cups COOKED VEGETABLES

Cook and stir ground beef and onion in Dutch oven until beef is brown; drain. Stir in sauce mix, water, Bay lead, salt, pepper and tomatoes (with liquid); break up tomatoes with fork - heat to boiling, stirring constantly. Reduce heat, cover and simmer, stirring occasionally for 10 minutes. Stir in noodles and vegetables. Cover and cook 10 minutes longer. Serve in Bean Pot. Serves 5 or 6.

Bean Pot Enchiladas

Submitted by Shelley Hermann, OH

1 lb. GROUND BEEF	1 cup chopped ONION
1/2 chopped GREEN PEPPER	1 can BLACK BEANS

1 can PINTO / KIDNEY BEANS (drained)

1 can diced TOMATOES	1/3 cup WATER
1 tsp. CHILI POWDER	1/2 tsp. CUMIN
1/2 tsp. SALT	1/4 tsp. pepper

1 cup shredded monterey jack cheese & 1 cup sharp cheddar cheese
6 flour tortillas

In batter bowl, brown ground beef, onion and green pepper. Add the next 8 ingredients. Heat on high for 2-3 minutes. Simmer for 5 minutes. Combine cheeses. In bean pot, layer about 3/4 cup beef mixture, one tortilla and about 1/3 cup cheese. Repeat layers. Cover and cook in oven on low for 2-3 hours. Great served with sour cream.

Pot Roast

Submitted by Kathleen Botner, KY

1 med. BEEF ROAST
1 pkg. DRY ONION SOUP
4 CARROT STICKS
6 POTATOES
2 cups WATER (add more if needed)
1/4 teaspoon SALT
1/8 teaspoon PEPPER

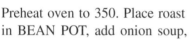

Preheat oven to 350. Place roast
in BEAN POT, add onion soup,
salt, pepper & water. Cook for 1 hour. Cut up carrots and potatoes.
Place carrots and potatoes with roast in bean pot. Bake for another
hour or until roast and vegetables are tender. Servings 4-6.

Ken's Spinach Casserole

Submitted by Ken Kiser, ID

4 - 10 oz. boxes frozen, chopped SPINACH, boiled and drained
1 pint SOUR CREAM
1 cup GRAPENUTS CEREAL (if runny more)
FRESH MUSHROOMS
PURPLE ONIONS (sautéed and drained)
1 pkg. of LIPTONS ONION SOUP MIX

Mix all items in Home & Garden Party 9x13 Baker. Top with lots of
cheddar cheese. Bake at 350 degrees 30 mins.

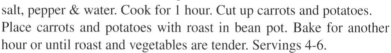

Hillbilly Beans

Submitted by Teresa K. Danielson, ID

1 lb HAMBURGER, browned and drained

1 large ONION, chopped	1/2 cup CELERY, chopped
3/4 cup BROWN SUGAR	2-3 tsp. PREPARED MUSTARD
1 can TOMATO SOUP	2 - 6 oz. can TOMATO PASTE
1 can PORK AND BEANS	1 can CHILLI BEANS
1 can GREEN BEANS, drained	1 can WAX BEANS, drained
1 can LIMA BEANS, drained	

Mix in large mixing bowl until all ingredients are incorporated. Pour into home and garden party bean pot. Mixture will fill completely to the top.

Lay bacon slices on top for garnish. Bake uncovered for 1 1/2 hours at 350°f.

Cabbage Casserole

Submitted by Dawne Kline, OH

2 lb. CABBAGE
SALT & PEPPER
1/4 lb. VELVETTA CHEESE
1 cup. MILK

Shred cabbage, put in skillet with a little water, simmer until tender, drain. Season with salt and pepper. In sauce pan combine milk, cheese and cornstarch. Stir until thickened. Mix good with cabbage. Put in covered casserole dish. Fix stuffing according to box. Spread on top of cabbage. Put in oven for 350 degrees for 30 minutes.

Trash Can Soup

Submitted by Crystal Dunt, MI

2 8 oz. cans of V-8
2 8 oz. cans of SPICY V-8
1 can of CORN
1 can of PEAS
1 can of diced CARROTS
1 can of BEEF BROTH
1 pkg. of ONION SOUP MIX
1 pkg. of COCKTAIL WEINERS
MONTEREY JACK CHEESE

Mix all ingredients except for Monterey Jack Cheese into the Home & Garden Party Bean Pot. Heat in oven at 350 for 30-45 minutes. Serve over cubed Monterey Jack Cheese in the Home & Garden Party Soup Bowls or Cereal Bowls.

Easy Baked Beans

Submitted by Penny Carlile, TX

2 16-18 oz. cans PORK AND BEANS
3/4 cup BROWN SUGAR
1 teaspoon DRY MUSTARD
6 slices BACON cut in pieces
1/2 cup KETCHUP

Empty 1/2 of the beans in buttered 7 x 11 Home & Garden Party casserole dish. Combine the brown sugar and the dry mustard, and sprinkle half of this mixture over the beans. Top with the remaining beans, and sprinkle the rest of the sugar/mustard mixture over the beans. Add the bacon pieces and the ketchup. Bake about 2 hours at 350 degrees.

Cheese Grits

Submitted by Penny Carlile, TX

1 cup GRITS
1 teaspoon SALT
3 cups boiling WATER
1 stick BUTTER OR MARGARINE
1 stick SHARP CHEESE cut in small pieces
2 well beaten EGGS
1/2 cup MILK

Stir grits into the boiling water. Add butter and cheese. Cook until blended. Add eggs and milk and bake in a 9x13 Baker at 325 degrees until done.

Entrees

Barbecued Pork

Submitted by Helen Holthaus, OH

2 -3 lbs. PORK ROAST
1 can COCA COLA
2 cups KETCHUP
1 ONION chopped

Place pork roast in Bean Pot, cover with chopped onion, then pour coke cola over the top and next pour ketchup over. Place lid on pot and bake in 400° over 2 1/2 - 3 hours (till meat is done) Meat will be tender enough to spread with fork while stirring the sauce all through the pork. You can use beef roast or turkey breast instead of the pork.

Coke Roast

Submitted by Helen Holthaus, OH

2 -3 lb. BEEF ROAST
1 can COKE COLA
1 can CREAM MUSHROOM SOUP (cream celery is good too)

Place roast in Bean Pot and then coke and cream soup, cover and bake 2 1/2 -3 hours at 400° Makes great gravy.
Great Variations: use pork or turkey breast and your favorite cream soup. You can also add carrots, celery and potatoes for pot roast dinner!

Pizza Casserole

Submitted by Dawne Kline, OH

(Kids love this one)

1 1/2 lbs. browned HAMBURGER	24 oz. MOZZARELLA CHEESE
1 chopped ONION	1 pkg. PEPPERONI
1 can MUSHROOM SOUP	2 cans PIZZA SAUCE
2/3 box RIGATONI MACARONI (cooked)	

Alternate layers in 9x13 baker. Hamburger, macaroni, cheese, soup, onion, pizza sauce and pepperoni.
Bake at 350 degrees 25-30 minutes.

Company Chicken Noodle Casserole

Submitted by Carolyn Yonchuk, PA

1/2 cup MAYONNAISE	2 tbsp LEMON JUICE
2 cups cubed cooked CHICKEN	1 small ONION, chopped

1/4 cup chopped GREEN PEPPER
1/4 cup chopped SWEET RED PEPPER
NOODLES, cooked and drained
1 cup shredded MONTEREY JACK (divided)
1 cup shredded SHARP CHEDDAR (divided)
12 ounces medium EGG

In a large bowl, combine soup, mayonnaise and lemon juice. Add the chicken, onion, peppers, 1/2 cup each of the cheeses; mix well. Add noodles and toss to coat, Transfer to 9x13 baker. Bake uncovered at 350 degrees for 30-35 minutes. Sprinkle with remaining cheeses. Bake 10 minutes longer or until vegetables are tender and cheese is melted. Serves 6.

"Picture Perfect" Baked Chicken

Submitted by Kathie Van Loon, MI

9x13 BAKING STONE 1/2 pkg. ONION SOUP MIX
6 - 8 CHICKEN BREASTS
1 8 oz. bottle FRENCH DRESSING (creamy orange style)
1 can whole CRANBERRY SAUCE (Ocean Spray)

Arrange chicken breasts in "seasoned" baker. Mix other ingredients together and spoon over the meat. Bake uncovered at 375 degrees approximately 1 hour.

Chicken Supreme

Submitted by Annie Allen, KS

6 CHICKEN BREAST halves
1 teaspoon or **1 cube** of **CHICKEN BULLION**
1/2 cup HOT WATER (dissolve chicken bullion in hot water)
1/2 cup WHITE WINE (optional- alcohol will cook off)
1 small can sliced MUSHROOMS w/ liquid
Pour liquids over breast placed in rectangular Baker.

Season Chicken Breast with the following spices:

3/4 tsp. SEASON SALT	**1 tsp. PAPRIKA**
1/2 tsp. CURRY POWDER	**1/4 tsp. PARSLEY FLAKES**
1/2 tsp. POULTRY SEASONING	**SALT AND PEPPER**

1 Tablespoon DRIED MINCED ONION
    or **1/4 cup fresh chopped Onion**

Cover with foil and bake at 375 degrees for 45-60 minutes. Remove from oven, place breasts on a serving Platter. Combine 1 Tablespoon Cornstarch and 2 Tablespoons COLD water to form a smooth milky paste. Combine with liquids remaining in Baker for a demi-gloss glaze to pour over Chicken Breast. Serves 6.

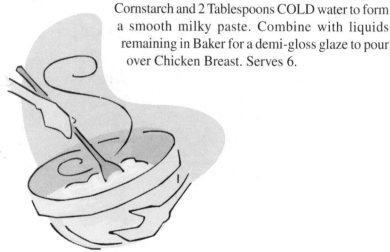

Chicken Cordon Bleu

Submitted by Cindy Welsh, PA

BEAN POT
6 skinned and boned CHICKEN BREASTS
6 slices cooked lean HAM
6 slices CHEESE (low fat swiss tastes great)
1 EGG beaten
1/4 cup ALL PURPOSE FLOUR
VEGETABLE COOKING SPRAY
1/2 cup chopped ONION
1 can (10 1/2 oz.) CREAM OF CHICKEN SOUP
Optional: TOASTED ALMONDS or TOASTED BREAD CRUMBS

1. Place chicken pieces on a cutting board and pound with a wooden mallet. Work from the center out pounding to make the breasts approximately 1/4 inch thick.
2. Flatten the breast and place a ham slice on top, then, a slice of cheese. Tuck in the sides and roll up as a jelly roll. Skewer or tie together.
3. Dip the chicken roll in egg, dredge in flour and then place seam side down in the BEAN POT.
4. Combine onion and soup. Pour over chicken and cover with lid.
5. Bake 350 degrees for 1 hour or until done and tender. (time may vary due to size of chicken breast.
6. Garnish with toasted almonds or toasted bread crumbs and serve. Serves 6.

One Dish Ham BBQ

Submitted by Cindy Welsh, PA

BEAN POT
1 tablespoon VINEGAR
1 cup favorite BBQ SAUCE
2 1/2 lbs. cooked or chopped HAM (sliced or shaved)

3 tablespoons BROWN SUGAR
1 cup KETCHUP

1. Mix first four ingredients together in the BEAN POT.
2. Cut ham in small pieces, then mix with BBQ sauce in the BEAN POT.
3. Wipe top and sides of BEAN POT.
4. Bake 350 degrees 1 hour
5. Serve - spoon out of the BEAN POT into rolls.

One Dish BBQ Ribs

Submitted by Cindy Welsh, PA

5 tablespoons DARK BROWN SUGAR   1/2 tablespoon VINEGAR
3 1/2 pounds PORK RIBS   1 1/2 cup KETCHUP
1 1/2 teaspoon LIQUID HICKORY SMOKE SEASONING
BEAN POT

1. Mix first four ingredients together, reserving 1/2 cup for later use.
2. One at a time stir the ribs into the BBQ sauce in the BEAN POT. Mix to coat evenly.
3. Wipe top and sides of BEAN POT.
4. Bake 325 degrees 3 1/3 hour or until tender. This makes a great meal to start before a meeting or church. When arriving home:
5. Drain sauce and grease from BEAN POT, pour reserved BBQ sauce over ribs and place in oven at 350 degrees 15 minutes. This gives you time to set the table and whip up a salad and potato.
6. Serve - out of the BEAN POT.

Impossible Chicken Quesadilla Pie

Submitted by Catherine Alton, CA

1 to 4 cans (4 oz) chopped GREEN CHILIS-according to your taste
8 c shredded CHEDDAR OR MIXED CHEESES
1 to 2 cups cooked and SHREDDED CHICKEN
3 c MILK
2 c BAKING MIX (like Bisquick)
8 EGGS

Heat oven to 425 degrees. Sprinkle chilis, cheeses and chicken in bottom of 9x13 Baker. Beat remaining ingredients until smooth, 15 to 30 seconds in a blender on high. Pour into baker. Bake until knife inserted into center comes out clean, 30 to 45 minutes. Cool 10 minutes. Serve with sour cream and guacamole. Serves 8 to 12.

Chow Mein Hotdish

Submitted by Kim Miller, WI

1 & 1/2 lbs. HAMBURGER	CELERY & ONIONS
1/4 cup SOY SAUCE	2 cans CHICKEN NOODLE SOUP
1 can CREAM OF MUSHROOM SOUP	
1 cup RICE uncooked	2 soup cans WATER
1/2 tsp. SALT	

Mix. Bake 1 & 1/2 hours at 350 degrees. After baking one hour sprinkle with Chow Mein noodles. Then bake the rest of the time.

Caribbean Chicken

Submitted by Tina De Villez, IN

4 unbreaded CHICKEN BREAST filets (thawed)
1/2 cup chopped ONION
2 tablespoons GARLIC POWDER
1/2 cup chopped GREEN PEPPER
1/2 teaspoon SALT & PEPPER
3 tablespoons LEMON JUICE
1/3 cup VEGETABLE OIL

In mixing bowl, mix all ingredients and add chicken. Cover & refrigerate at least 4 hours. Remove chicken and place in Chip & Dip. Take liquid mixture and pour over chicken. Bake uncovered at 350 degrees for approximately one hour or until chicken is done.

El Rancho Chicken

Submitted by Debbie Lagerhausen, IL

2 whole CHICKEN BREASTS (halved, boned & skinned)
1/2 cup refrigerated BUTTERMILK SALAD DRESSING mix
    (Hidden Valley)
1-1/4 cups crushed NACHO CHEESE CHIPS

*Preheat oven to 350 degrees
*Lightly spray Baking Stone w/ cooking oil
*Pound Chicken alittle
*Dip into dressing, then roll into crushed chips.
*Place on Stone
*Bake 30-40 minutes

Great served with Salsa, corn w/sweet peppers & black olives.

Mexican Lasagna

Submitted by Patricia Ingersoll, UT

1 lb. GROUND BEEF
1/2 lb. GROUND PORK
1 small ONION, chopped
1 1/2 cups SALSA
1 teaspoon GARLIC POWDER
2 cups frozen WHITE CORN
1 cup canned BLACK BEANS
1 8 oz. can TOMATO SAUCE
1 large RED PEPPER, diced
1 tablespoon LIME JUICE
12 WHITE CORN TORTILLAS
1 cup SOUR CREAM
1 cup slice OLIVES
1 1/2 cups grated JACK CHEESE
1 cup shredded LETTUCE

Brown meat, add onion and cook until tender. Add garlic powder, salsa, corn, tomato sauce, beans, peppers, lime juice and olives. Simmer uncovered 15 min., stirring occasionally. In the 9x13 Home & Garden Party baker, layer 6 tortillas, overlap if needed. Top with 1/2 of the meat mixture. Top with remaining 6 tortillas, spread with sour cream, top with remaining meat mixture and grated cheese. Bake at 350 degrees for 30 min. Remove from oven and let stand for 10min. Cut into squares, serve with lettuce on top.

Chicken Casserole

Submitted by Treva Castleberry, TN

4 large CHICKEN BREASTS (cut up into bite size cubes)
1 pkg. PEPPERIDGE FARM HERBED STUFFING MIX
1 can CREAM OF BROCCOLI SOUP
1 can of CREAM OF CHICKEN SOUP
1 8 oz. container of SOUR CREAM
1 stick of BUTTER

Saute the chicken breasts in a skillet sprinkling with garlic salt until the meat is pre-cooked. Combine the soup and sour cream. Place the chicken in our Home & Garden Party 9x13 baker, that has been sprayed with Pam cooking spray. Pour the soup/sour cream mixture over the chicken. Spread the stuffing mix evenly over the chicken and soup mixture. Melt the stick of butter and pour it over the stuffing mix. Place the baker in the oven on approx. 350 degrees for one hour. This is one of my family's favorite recipes.

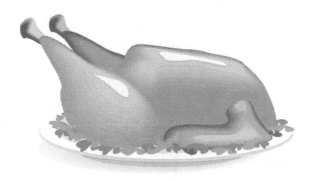

My Favorite Pasta Casserole

Submitted by Kathleen Axsom, IN

6-8 cups of COOKED PASTA
  (I like to use the pretty colorful ones, but any type will do)
1 envelope of your favorite SPAGHETTI SAUCE or TACO SAUCE mix.
1 1/2 pounds of cooked GROUND BEEF
  (Add the envelope of sauce mix while cooking your ground beef)
2 cans of DICED TOMATOES (12-14oz.) size
1 can TOMATO PASTE (4-6 oz.) size
1 bunch of GREEN ONIONS (chopped) can substitute regular onions
1 & 1/2 cups your choice of CHEDDAR, or COLBY CHEESE
  (cubed or chopped)

Mix all above ingredients well in Home & Garden Party's mixing bowl, then bake at 325 degrees in your Home & Garden Party's Casserole Dish OR your Home & Garden Party's Bean Pot for approx. 20 min or until cheese is melted.

Add your favorite bread and tossed salad and you have a quick and tasty meal in less than 30 min. This recipe can be adjusted easily to suit your own taste.

Country Fried Steak

Submitted by Martha West, SC

STEAK, chopped or cubed
MARGARINE
1 can MUSHROOM SOUP
1 ONION, sliced

SALT
PEPPER
FLOUR

Salt and pepper steak, roll in flour. Melt margarine in skillet and brown on both sides. Place steak in 9x13 Baker.

Make gravy by combining mushroom soup, 2 cans of water and 1 sliced onion in a saucepan; bring to a boil.

Pour gravy over steak and cover with heavy aluminum foil.

Bake @ 350 degrees for 1 1/2 hours.

I have used both of these recipes for years, but I have not actually used them in the 12" Pie Plate or the 9x13" Baker since both of these are new items. You may have to experiment with different dishes.

Amazing Meat Loaf

Submitted by Michele Ault, OH

1 1/2 pounds lean HAMBURGER
1/2 c. MILK
1 EGG
1/2 c. BROWN SUGAR
1/2 tsp. DRY MUSTARD
1 clove GARLIC, crushed
1 tbsp. WORCESTERSHIRE SAUCE

1 1/4 c. dry BREAD CRUMBS
3/4 c. BARBECUE SAUCE
1/3 c. chopped ONION
1 1/2 tsp. SEASONED SALT
1/4 tsp. PEPPER

Mix all ingredients and spread in a loaf pan. Bake uncovered in a 350° oven until done, about 1 1/2 hours. 6 Servings.

Meat Pie

Submitted by Cindy Bower, IL

1 lb. GROUND BEEF	4 oz. can - drained MUSHROOMS
1 EGG	1/3 c. chopped ONION
dry BREAD CRUMBS	

Combine meat, mushrooms, egg, onion, bread crumbs and a dash of salt & pepper. Mix well. Press into the pie plate as the "crust". Bake at 400 degrees for about 45 minutes. When done, drain.

2 c chopped, cooked POTATOES
3 tsb. MILK
1/2 lb. CHEESE

While meat is cooking, cook the potatoes. Drain and mash with the 3 tablespoons of milk and stir in the cheese. Fill the meat shell with the cheesy potatoes. Bake at 350° degrees for 10 minutes.

Marlene's Cornbread Taco Bake

Submitted by Marlene Cox, PA

This recipes works great in the Home & Garden Party Casserole Dish (uncovered). You can use it in the Flower Pot also and it will be filled to the top.

1 1/2 pounds chopped MEAT OR TURKEY
1 package TACO SEASONING MIX
1/2 cup WATER
1 (12 oz) can drained CORN
1/2 cup chopped GREEN PEPPER
1 (8 oz) can TOMATO SAUCE
1/2 can small can "DURKEE FRENCH FRIED ONIONS"
1 (8 1/2 oz) package JIFFY CORNBREAD MUFFIN MIX
1/3 cup shredded CHEESE (cheddar or jack works best)

In skillet, brown meat or turkey, Drain. Stir in taco seasoning, water, corn, pepper, and tomato sauce. Pour into Home & Garden Party's Casserole Dish. In Home & Garden Party's Mixing Bowl, prepare corn bread mix according to package directions. Spread cornbread mixture over the top of meat mixture completely and evenly. Place french fried onions on top. Bake UNCOVERED 400° for 20 mins. Top with 1/3 cup cheese. Bake 3 mins more until cheese, is completely melted. Great to serve with tortilla chips.

Pork Noodle Casserole

Submitted by Deb Wolf, IA

Combine and mix in a greased casserole:

Cooked & drained NOODLES

1 pound lean, cooked PORK (leftover pork roast works great)

1 cup diced VELVEETA CHEESE

1 can CREAM OF MUSHROOM SOUP with 1/2 CAN MILK

1/2 cup chopped SALAD OLIVES or PIMENTOS

1 - 4 ounce can of MUSHROOM STEMS & PIECES (drained)

Top with 2 cups crushed potato chips.

Microwave on high for about 7 minutes or bake @ 350° for 35 minutes.

Lasagna

Submitted by Linda Jenkins-Schneider, OH

Necessary for a perfect flavor: One Home & Garden Party's Bakeware 13x9 Baker

Fry 2 lbs. GROUND CHUCK (drain)
Add and cook 5-10 minutes:

3 cloves of GARLIC (crushed)	**18 oz. can TOMATO PASTE**
1/2 can of WATER	**1 1/2 tablespoons PARSLEY**
1 1/2 teaspoons BLACK PEPPER	**1 tablespoon SALT**

pinch OREGANO (or a nice shake is okay, too)
dash of PEPPER SEEDS (optional)

Add:

1 large can TOMATO PUREE	**2/3 can WATER**
1 teaspoon SUGAR	

Cook 1 1/2 hours or until sauce is no longer runny. It should sit on top of itself. Add 1/4 cup Romano cheese.

Boil 9 lasagna noodles 15 minutes. Should be slightly firm, but not hard. Drain. Lay noodles flat to dry.

Combine and mix thoroughly with a spoon:

1 1/2 lbs. RICOTTA CHEESE (let stand for 1 hour before using)	
1 cup ROMANO CHEESE	**5 EGGS**
2 teaspoons SALT	**1/3 cup PARSLEY**

In Home & Garden Party's 13x9 Baker:
Pour sauce just to cover bottom. Add 3 noodles side by side. Add 1/2 of Ricotta cheese mixture, and spread evenly. The drier the noodles, the easier this is. Add generous sprinkle of shredded Mozarella cheese. Repeat.
End top with 3 noodles, sauce, Romano cheese.
Bake at 350 degrees for 30 minutes. DO NOT COVER.

Home & Garden Party's Heavenly Hamburger Delight

Submitted by Judy Schaff, NV

Will need Home & Garden Party's 9x13 Baker

2 tablespoons OLEO
1 clove GARLIC
dash of PEPPER
2 cans TOMATO SAUCE (8 oz. each)
1 package CREAM CHEESE (3 oz.)
6 GREEN ONIONS, chopped with green tops
1/2 cup grated CHEESE (CHEDDAR)
1 package NOODLES (8 oz.)

1 pound of HAMBURGER
1 teaspoon SALT
1 teaspoon SUGAR
1 cup SOUR CREAM

Melt oleo in skillet; add hamburger and garlic. Brown. Add salt, pepper, sugar and tomato sauce. Lower heat and simmer covered for 20 minutes. Soften cream cheese and mix with sour cream and green onions. Cook noodles and drain. Put layer of noodles, then onion mix, then hamburger mixture in a 9x13 Baker. Repeat once again with layers and add grated cheese on top. Bake at 350 degrees in oven for 20 minutes.

Taco Pizza Pie

Submitted by Melissa Weltz, OH

1 tube of CRESCENT DINNER ROLLS
1 1/2 lb. GROUND BEEF
1 pkg. TACO SEASONING and water (as directed on pkg.)
1 cup DORITO CHIPS (crushed)
1 cup shredded CHEDDAR CHEESE

Preheat oven to 350°. Spread rolls out on Home & Garden Party's round baking stone to form pizza crust. Brown ground beef and drain excess fat. Add taco seasoning and water as directed on package. Spread crushed Doritos over rolls and then add meat mixture. Top with cheese. Bake 30 minutes.

Pork Chops & Rice

Submitted by Ruthann Martinez, AZ

Empty contents of purchased rice/pilaf mix (Uncle Ben's or Near East) into Bean Pot. Add water according to package directions. Place pork chops on top of rice and sprinkle seasoning mix on meat. Cover and bake for 1-2 hours at 350°F.

Sausage & Pepperoni Pizza Casserole

Submitted by Judy Gunter, VA

1 1/2 - 2 lbs. of SAUSAGE
12 oz. -16 oz. WIDE NOODLES, cooked according to package directions
2 (14 oz.) jars PIZZA SAUCE
3-4 cups shredded CHEDDAR CHEESE
12 oz. sliced PEPPERONI

Preheat oven to 350 degrees.

Crumble sausage into medium skillet; cook over medium heat until brown, stirring occassionally.

Remove sausage and drain on paper towels. In 9x13 BAKEWARE (99176) baker,(if bakeware is not seasoned, you might want to spray inside with vegetable spray) .... layer 1/2 of noodles, 1/2 of sausage, and 1/2 of remaining ingredients. Repeat with second layer of noodles, then sausage and remaining ingredients, reserving several pepperoni slices to garnish top, Bake 40 - 45 minutes depending on your oven. Serve immediately. Refrigerate leftovers. Serves 6 -10 folks. You can 1/2 the recipe and cook in the Chip n' Dip (99350). Children love this…

Chicken with Stuffing Casserole

Submitted by Emily Allison, VA

2 pkg. STOVE TOP STUFFING
2 10 oz. cans of CHUNKY CHICKEN drained
3/4 c. MILK
1 can CREAM OF MUSHROOM SOUP
2 cans CREAM OF CHICKEN SOUP

Prepare stuffing according to package instructions. Coat 9 x 13 bakeware dish with vegetable spray. Pat stuffing in bakeware dish. Sprinkle chicken on top of stuffing. Mix soups and milk until smooth, pour over chicken. Cover with aluminum foil. Bake at 350 degrees for 45 minutes.

Hot Chicken Salad

Submitted by Thelma Jenkins, NY

1 to 2 lbs. CHICKEN
1 can CREAM OF CHICKEN SOUP
1 cup of MAYO
3 hard boiled EGGS (chopped)
1/2 cup of chopped ONIONS
1 cup of grated CHEESE
1 cup of crushed POTATO CHIPS

Cook chicken and cut in small chunks. Mix soup, Mayo, eggs, onions. Then add chicken and put mixture in Bean Pot.
Mix chips and cheese together and put over top mixture. Cook 350° for 45 minutes with cover on.

Chuck Roast with Gravy

Submitted by Ruthann Martinez, AZ

1 can ROASTED GARLIC CREAM OF MUSHROOM SOUP
1 can COKE
OR
1 can CREAM OF MUSHROOM SOUP
1 pkg. LIPTON'S ONION SOUP MIX
1 can COKE

Place roast and other ingredients in Bean Pot. Cover with the lid. Bake in 350°F oven for about 2 hours.

Chicken Caesar Pizza

Submitted by Sandy Boeckman, IA

Chicken Caesar Pizza is another great hit at the show!

Pan bake a **PIZZA CRUST** or French bread loaf on the round stone for 10 minutes at 350 degrees.
Spread a layer of Caesar Salad Dressing on top.
Layer diced up chicken, onion and lots of pizza cheese on top of dressing.
Bake until cheese melts or turns golden brown for about 11 minutes at 350 degrees.
Top your pizza with chopped up lettuce, more dressing and bacon bits!

White Chili

Submitted by Ronda Ericson-Eggerling, NE

2 pounds GREAT NORTHERN BEANS
4 cans CHICKEN BROTH
1 ONION, chopped
2 cloves GARLIC, minced
1 tablespoon DRIED OREGANO, crushed
1 1/2 tablespoon ground CUMIN
1 teaspoon ground RED PEPPER (CAYENNE)
4 chopped cooked CHICKEN BREASTS
16 oz. SOUR CREAM
1 lb. MONTEREY JACK CHEESE, shredded

1. Soak beans overnight. Drain and rinse. Cook beans in fresh water. Drain water from beans
2. Combine beans, broth, onion, garlic, oregano, cumin, red pepper, 1/2 teaspoon salt and 1/2 teaspoon pepper. Bring to boiling. Reduce heat. Cover and simmer 1/2 hour.
3. Stir in the chicken and sour cream. Simmer, covered, for 1/2 hour more. Before serving, stir in the cheese till just melted. Do not bring to a boil after adding cheese or it will clump.

Chicken Crunch

Submitted by Gloria Alexander, KY

3 cups cooked CHICKEN, cut into bite size pieces
3/4 cups MAYONNAISE
3 cups chopped CELERY
1/2 cups chopped GREEN PEPPER
2 tablespoons chopped PIMENTOS
3 tablespoon LEMON JUICE
1 can CREAM OF CHICKEN SOUP
1 can chopped WATER CHESTNUTS
3/4 teaspoon SALT
3 tablespoon grated ONION

Combine all above in Home & Garden Party's Mixing Bowl, toss lightly and spoon into Home & Garden Party's 9x13 Baker.

1/4 cup chopped ALMONDS
3/4 cup grated CHEESE (the kind you put on spaghetti)
3 cups crushed POTATO CHIPS

Crush chips in plastic bag; add almonds and cheese. Shake to mix together. Top casserole with mixture and bake in 350 degree oven for 25 minutes.
I serve this casserole over medium noodles.

Spaghetti Crusted Turkey Pie

Submitted by Reeva Leahy, WA

6 ounces of SPAGHETTI uncooked
2 EGGS beaten
1/3 cup grated PARMESAN CHEESE
2/3 cup SOUR CREAM
1 tablespoon BUTTER OR MARGARINE
1 package 1 one-fourth GROUND TURKEY (can sub. beef)
3/4 cup GREEN PEPPER
1/3 cup chopped ONION
1 8 ounce TOMATO SAUCE
1 teaspoon GARLIC SALT
4 ounces sliced MOZZARELLA CHEESE

Spray Pam in pie pan, break spaghetti into halves. Cook in boiling water until tender, drain, mix eggs, Parmesan cheese and warm spaghetti. Pour into pie pan. Pat in bottom and up sides of pie plate with back of spoon. Spread sour cream over the bottom.

Heat oven to 350 degrees. Heat butter in large skillet over medium heat until melted. Crumble turkey into skillet; stir in green pepper and onion. Cook until turkey is no longer pink, drain. Sir in tomato sauce, garlic salt. Simmer for 10 minutes. Salt and pepper to taste. Spoon turkey mixture over sour cream. Bake 25 min. Arrange Mozzarella cheese on top. Bake until cheese is melted. Servings 6-7.

Beef and Sausage Casserole

Submitted by June Trask, KS

1 1/2 lbs of GROUND BEEF
1/2 pound JIMMY DEAN HOT SAUSAGE
12 CRACKERS (any kind)
1 small can ITALIAN TOMATO PASTE
1 bottle HEINZ CHILI SAUCE
1 1/2 tsp. OREGANO SALT
1 1/2 tsp. GARLIC SALT
1 EGG
1 medium ONION, chopped
1 8 oz. block of MONTEREY AND JACK CHEESE WITH JALAPENOS

In mixing bowl mix together all ingredients except for chili sauce. In your 9x13 baker take half of mixture and form a one layer loaf, take your cheese and lay out in slices on top. Then take remaining mixture and form top layer. Bake at 350° for 1 hour, take out and pour on chili sauce. Bake for another 20-30 minutes. Slice, serve and enjoy! Great served with a ranch pasta salad.

Easy Tuna Casserole

Submitted by Tonia Oda, OH

6 1/2 oz. can of TUNA   2/3 cup MILK
can of CREAM OF MUSHROOM or CELERY SOUP
2 cups MACARONI, cooked
1/4 cup ONIONS, diced
1 cup shredded cheese, COLBY OR CHEDDAR

Place all ingredients in Home & Garden Party's Casserole Dish and stir gently. Bake uncovered at 375 degrees for 30 minutes.

Forgotten Chicken

Submitted by Raelene Decker, PA

1 cup uncooked RICE (regular)
1 pkg. DRY ONION SOUP MIX
1 can CREAM OF MUSHROOM SOUP
1 can CREAM OF CELERY SOUP
1 soup can WATER
1 good sized CHICKEN-cooked & cut up in small pieces

Put rice in the bottom of the Home & Garden Party 9x13 Baker. Lay chicken pieces on top. Sprinkle with dry onion soup mix. Mix soups with water and heat. Pour over other ingredients already in the pan. Cover tightly with foil, DO NOT REMOVE WHILE COOKING! Bake at 325 degrees for 1 1/2 hours.
This is so simple and a meal in itself. It can be made ahead of time and frozen as well. I always come home with an empty dish when I take this to covered dish functions!

Chicken Divan

Submitted by Cathie Cordell, PA

(Baked in the Bean Pot)
2 10 oz. pkg. chopped BROCCOLI
1 can CREAM OF CHICKEN SOUP
2 t. LEMON JUICE
1/2 cup SHREDDED CHEESE
T BUTTER or MARGARINE

2 cups chopped CHICKEN
1/2 cup MAYONNAISE
1/2 t. PAPRIKA
1/2 cup CORNFLAKE crumbs

Cook broccoli and drain. Place in Bean Pot, sprayed with Pam. Place chicken on top of broccoli. Combine soup, mayonnaise, lemon juice, and paprika. Pour over and sprinkle with cheese, corn flake crumbs, and butter. Bake at 350 degrees for 25 to 30 minutes.

Anthing Goes Casserole Ring

Submitted by Lynn Leusch, CA

Using one of our beautiful Chip and Dip Pottery pieces, arrange 2 cans crescent triangles in a circular pattern with the points to the outside and the bases overlapping. This will form a "wreath" look when completed. Chop all ingredients and mix together. Spoon filling over base of crescent pieces. Fold points of triangle over filling and tuck under base at center. Bake 375° for 25-30 minutes or until golden brown.

*CHICKEN FILLING:
1 can cream of chicken soup, 1 c grated jack cheese, 1 can drained chicken, 1 cup broccoli (frozen or fresh), 2-4 green onions.
Optionals: water chestnuts, chopped canned green chilis, cheddar cheese, pepper jack cheese, regular onion, cream of celery soup, fresh pre-cooked chicken or many other meats work well.

*TACO FILLING: 1 16 oz. can refried beans, 1 1/2 lb. ground beef or turkey with taco seasonings, 1 can sliced olives, 2 cups grated cheddar cheese. Optionals: serve with all taco "goodies" such as lettuce, tomato, onion, guacamole.

*BROCCOLI HAM FILLING: 1 pre-cooked ham slice, 2 cups broccoli (frozen or fresh), 1 sm onion, 1 cup grated swiss cheese, 2 tbsp. Dijon mustard, 1 tsp lemon juice.

This is an "Anything Goes Casserole", because I just use my imagination with combinations of food and it all tastes great. Works well with leftovers. I always make a double recipe and there are never any leftovers. It's that yummy.

Rice Dish

Submitted by Wilma Stillwell, IL

Use the casserole dish.
Mix 2 1/4 cups MINUTE RICE
1 can CAMPBELL'S CONSOMME
Mix, then add:
1/2 stick OLEO (just lay on top of mixture)
Put in the microwave on high for 7 minutes.
Makes a great substitute for a potato with any meal.

Easy Pizza

Submitted by Wilma Stillwell, IL

Use the 9 x 13 stoneware pan.
1 pkg. of CRESCENT ROLLS spread across the complete bottom of pan.
2 teaspoons of a SPICY MUSTARD (optional) spread on top of crescents
1/2 cup CHILI SAUCE (or enough till lightly covered)
add one pound of cooked crumbled GROUND BEEF
sprinkle CHILI POWDER to taste
Top with 8 ounces of shredded CHEDDAR CHEESE

Bake at 350° degrees till crust appears golden around the edges and the cheese is melted and maybe a little brown. Cut in squares and serve.

Broccoli and Chicken Braid

Submitted by Dawn Hall, VA

3 boneless skinless CHICKEN BREASTS (cooked and chopped)
1 cup BROCCOLI (cooked and chopped)
1 cup CHEDDAR CHEESE grated
1 1/2 cans CREAM SOUP (chicken, celery or mushroom). I like chicken.
GARLIC, SALT, and PEPPER to taste
2 cans refrigerated CRESCENT ROLLS

In Home & Garden Party's Mixing Bowl mix all ingredients well. On Home & Garden Party's Baking Stone (square or round) lay out the 2 pkgs. of rolls flat. Pinch perforations together until smooth. Spread mixture in center of dough. Loaf style. Take a knife and cut slits from the mixture out to the edge of the dough. Bring the cut pieces up to the center of the mix and pinch together. Brush lightly with melted margarine.
Bake 25-30 minutes at 350° or until dough is done. Serve warm—DELICIOUS!

Broccoli and Rice Casserole

Submitted by Dawn Hall, VA

1 head BROCCOLI, steamed and chopped
1 med. ONION, sauteed   1 cup cooked RICE
1 cup WATER   1 8 oz. CHEEZ WHIZ
2 cans CREAM OF CHICKEN SOUP
1 cup shredded CHEDDAR CHEESE

In Home & Garden Party's Mixing Bowl mix first ingredients well. Mix others in medium saucepan until cheeses melt. Mix all ingredients together well. Bake in 9x13 Stoneware Baker 45-50 minutes at 350°.

Chicken Divan

Submitted by Tonia Oda, OH

2 - 10 oz. pkgs. frozen BROCCOLI
3-4 boneless skinless CHICKEN BREASTS, cooked and sliced
2 cans CREAM OF CHICKEN SOUP
1 cup MAYONNAISE
pinch CURRY POWDER (very little)
1/2 cup shredded SHARP CHEESE
1 cup BREAD CRUMBS
1 Tbsp. melted MARGARINE
few drops LEMON JUICE

Cook broccoli until tender. Drain and arrange broccoli in 9x13 baker. Place chicken on top of broccoli. Combine soup, mayonnaise, lemon juice and curry powder in separate bowl and pour evenly over the chicken. Sprinkle with cheese. Combine bread crumbs and margarine; and sprinkle over all.
Bake in 375° degree oven for 30 to 45 minutes.

Brunch Pizza Squares

Submitted by Margie Elling, MI

1 pound BULK SAUSAGE
4 EGGS
2 tablespoons MILK
1/8 teaspoon PEPPER
3/4 cups shredded CHEDDAR CHEESE
1 (8 oz) tube refrigerated CRESCENT ROLLS

In a skillet brown sausage; drain. Unroll crescent rolls and spread in our lightly greased 9x13 stoneware baker. Press dough 1/2 inches up the sides and seal seams. Sprinkle sausage over dough. Beat eggs, milk and pepper; pour over sausage. Sprinkle with cheese. Bake uncovered at 400 degrees for 15 minutes or until crust is golden brown and cheese is melted.

Green Chili Enchiladas

Submitted by Kathy Cotterman, MN

1 - 1/2 lbs. lean GROUND BEEF or 3 3/4 c. CHICKEN
1 1/4 c. finely chopped ONION
1 T. CHILI POWDER
SALT AND PEPPER to taste
8-12 FLOUR TORTILLAS
3 c. MONTEREY JACK CHEESE, shredded
 (Reserve 1 c. cheese for top)
1 10 3/4 oz. can CREAM OF CHICKEN SOUP
1 1/2 c. SOUR CREAM
1 - 4 oz. can GREEN CHILIS, diced

Brown meat and onion, drain. Mix in chili powder, salt, pepper, and cheese. Fill each tortilla with mixture. Roll and place in 9x13 Baker, seam side down.
Mix together sour cream, soup and chilis. Pour over top of tortillas.
Baker 375° for 20-25 minutes. Last 10 minutes put remaining cup of cheese on top. Serve with tomato and lettuce if desired. Home & Garden uses mixing bowl, 9x13 Baker, cereal bowl, book rack for holding recipe book.

Bean Pot Chicken Pozole

Submitted by Lisa Israel, CA

This a great rainy-day dinner

2 lbs. CHICKEN BREASTS, legs, and thighs
2 tbsp OLIVE OIL
6 cloves GARLIC (or to personal taste), minced
1 large can HOMINY, drained
1 large ONION, chopped
1 large can (24 oz.) diced STEWED TOMATOES, with juice
        (the Mexican style ones works great for this)
CHICKEN BROTH to cover in bean pot, about 2 cups
1 tbsp. CUMIN or to taste
1 tsp. TABASCO or to taste (optional)
Salt and Pepper to taste
Topping:
Grated CHEDDAR CHEESE
Fresh CILANTRO LEAVES
SOUR CREAM
GUACAMOLE
JALAPENO RINGS
BLACK OLIVE, slices

Brown chicken in olive oil and garlic. Place in bean pot. Add hominy, onion, tomatoes, and seasonings. Add chicken broth to cover.
Place in 375 degree oven and cook 1 to 1-1/2 hours. Serve in our soup or cereal bowls. Pass toppings. Boneless/skinless chicken breasts can be used to make this ultra low-fat. Can also be used with diced pork roast. Serves 8.

Taco Crescents

Submitted by Ginny Blair, NY

These are easy to make, freeze well, too. Kids love'em!

3/4 pound GROUND BEEF
1/4 cup chopped ONION
1 package (1-1/4 ounces) TACO SEASONING
1 can (4-1/4 ounces) chopped RIPE OLIVES, drained
2 EGGS, lightly beaten
1/2 cup shredded CHEDDAR CHEESE
2 tubes (8 ounces each) refrigerated CRESCENT ROLLS

In skillet, brown beef with onion; drain. Add taco seasoning and olives, mix well and set aside to cool. Add eggs and cheese mixing well. On baking stone, separate dough. Place 2 tablespoons of meat mixture onto each triangle. Roll and shape into crescents. Bake at 375 degrees for 10 to 15 minutes or until lightly browned. Yield: 8 servings

Poor Man's Dinner

Submitted by Ginny Blair, NY

Don't let the name fool you- this dish guarantees a "million dollar taste"-
just a few ingredients and Oh! so good!!

1 to 1-1/2 pounds of GROUND BEEF
1/2 teaspoon PEPPER
1/4 teaspoon GARLIC POWDER
5 to 6 large POTATOES, peeled and sliced
1 large SWEET ONION, sliced
**2 cans (10 3/4 ozs. each) CONDENSED CREAM OF MUSHROOM SOUP,
     undiluted.**
Chopped fresh PARSLEY

In skillet brown ground beef; drain. Season with pepper and garlic
powder. Lightly spray bean pot with cooking spray and layer beef,
potatoes and onions (you will get three to four layers from above
ingredients). Pour soup over all. Cover and bake at 350 degrees for 1
hour or until potatoes are tender. Garnish with parsley.
Yield: 6 servings
Helpful hint! I place a piece of aluminum foil between the lid and pot
to help with spillovers and clean up.

CHEESY BEEF DINNER:
Substitute 2 cans (11 ozs. each) of condensed Cheddar cheese soup,
undiluted in place of the mushroom soup above and follow the same
recipe for a whole new taste.

Spaghetti Pizza

Submitted by Sandy Jackson, OH

1 box of SPAGHETTI
1 package sliced PEPPERONI
1 can SPAGHETTI SAUCE
1 package of shredded MOZZARELLA CHEESE

Cook the spaghetti according to package directions and drain. Place in a lightly greased 9x13 stoneware baker. Top with sliced pepperoni, then pour the sauce over all. Cover with Mozzarella cheese. Bake at 350° for about 30 minutes or until the cheese is melted and bubbly.

Li'l Cheddar Meat Loaves

Submitted by Sandy Jackson, OH

1 EGG
3/4 cup MILK
1 cup (4 oz.) shredded CHEDDAR CHEESE
1/2 cup QUICK COOKING OATS
1/2 cup chopped ONION
1/2 tsp. SALT
1 lb. lean GROUND BEEF
2/3 cup KETCHUP
1/2 cup packed BROWN SUGAR
1 1/2 tsp. PREPARED MUSTARD

In a bowl, beat the egg and milk. Stir in cheese, oats, onion and salt. Add the beef and mix well. Shape into eight small loaves, place in lightly greased 9x13 Baker. Combine ketchup, brown sugar and mustard; spoon over the loaves. Bake uncovered for 45 minutes at 350° or until the meat is no longer pink and a meat thermometer reads 160. Yields: 8 servings

Italian Veggie Salad

Submitted by Sandy Jackson, OH

1 cup sliced CARROTS
2 cups chopped BROCCOLI
1 cup chopped GREEN PEPPERS
2 cups chopped CAULIFLOWER
1 cup CELERY
1/2 cup chopped TOMATO
1 bottle ZESTY ITALIAN SALAD DRESSING (Kraft tastes the best).

The veggies are coated and serve in the mixing bowl pattern of your choice. This is a very festive salad because of the reds and greens. It is great to make up a day ahead in the covered casserole dish or bean pot because these veggies hold up real well in the dressing.

Louisiana Jambalaya

Submitted by Renee Lewis, LA

1 lb. SMOKED SAUSAGE
1 CHICKEN, boiled and deboned
1 stick MARGARINE
1 cup RICE
1/2 cup BELL PEPPER
1 can BEEF BROTH
1 can FRENCH ONION SOUP
1 soup can of WATER

Brown rice in margarine and then drain margarine. Add broth, soup and can of water. Cut sausage into bite size pieces. Mix all ingredients together and pour into Bean Pot. Bake at 350° degrees for 1 1/2 hours, stirring every thirty minutes.

Busy Day Chicken

Submitted by Renee Lewis, LA

2-3 lbs. CHICKEN pieces   **1 cup RICE, uncooked**
1 package DRY ONION SOUP MIX
1 can CREAM OF CELERY SOUP

Place rice in Bean Pot with chicken on top. Sprinkle with onion soup.
Mix celery soup and two cans of water; pour over the above. Bake with
lid on Bean Pot. Serves four to six.

Lasagna

Submitted by Linda Jenkins-Schneider, OH

Necessary for a perfect flavor: One Home & Garden Party's Bakeware Baker

Fry 2 lbs. ground chuck (drain)

Add and cook 5-10 minutes:

3 cloves of GARLIC (crushed)   **18 oz. can TOMATO PASTE**
1/2 can of WATER   **1 1/2 tablespoons PARSLEY**
1 1/2 teaspoons BLACK PEPPER   **1 tablespoon SALT**
pinch OREGANO (or a nice shake is okay, too)
dash of PEPPER SEEDS (optional)

Add:

1 large can TOMATO PUREE   **2/3 can WATER**
1 teaspoon SUGAR

Cook 1 1/2 hours or until sauce is no longer runny. It should sit on top of itself. Add 1/4 cup Romano cheese. Boil 9 lasagna noodles 15 minutes. Should be slightly firm, but not hard. Drain. Lay noodles flat to dry.

Combine and mix thoroughly with a spoon:

1 1/2 lbs. Ricotta cheese (let stand for 1 hour before using)
1 cup ROMANO CHEESE   **5 EGGS**
2 teaspoons SALT   **1/3 cup PARSLEY**

In Home & Garden Party Baker:
Pour sauce just to cover bottom. Add 3 noodles side by side. Add 1/2 of Ricotta cheese mixture, and spread evenly. The drier the noodles, the easier this is. Add generous sprinkle of shredded Mozzarella cheese. Repeat.
End top with 3 noodles, sauce, romano cheese.

Bake at 350 degrees for 30 minutes. DO NOT COVER

Unique Bean Pot
Roast Beef Dinner

Submitted by Lisa Kling, CO

(Or you can use beef roast, pork chops, ribs, and chicken.)

1 can DR. PEPPER   **1 c. KETCHUP**
4 t. WORCESTERSHIRE SAUCE   **3 t. dried BASIL**
2 t. GARLIC POWDER   **2 t. ONION POWDER**
4 POTATOES   **1 small ONION (optional)**
4 CARROTS, cut into coins

Beef Roast: Place a 2-3 lb. roast in your favorite BEAN POT and bake the roast at 300 degrees for 3 hours. Or leave out the veggies and break-up the roast and serve on sandwiches. (like a BBQ sandwich.)

Pork Chops or Chicken: Place 4 pork chops in our 9x13 stoneware dish and bake at 350 for 1 hr.

*Do not use Diet Dr. Pepper even if does taste the same. The sugar helps tenderize the meat.

Sensational Pork Chops

Submitted by Dee Hart, NE

6 center cut 1/2" PORK CHOPS
2 GRANNY SMITH APPLES, sliced & cored
1 medium ONION, sliced, rings separated
6 medium RED POTATOES
3 tbsp. VEGETABLE OIL
SALT, PEPPER & GARLIC POWDER to taste
1/4 cup WATER

Sprinkle each pork chop with salt, pepper & garlic powder. Heat oil in skillet and brown each pork chop briefly over high heat. Remove and place in bottom of Home & Garden Party's 9x13 Baker. Put 1/4 cup of water in skillet while hot, swirl around to collect drippings and pour over pork chops.

Layer remaining ingredients as follows: onion rings, sliced apples, onion rings, potatoes, onion rings & potatoes, sprinkling each layer lightly with salt, pepper & garlic powder. Cover snugly with aluminum foil and bake for 1 hour at 400 degrees.

Lee's Everything But, Meatloaf Meal

Submitted by Judy and Lee Smith, MI

3 lb. not too lean GROUND BEEF	3 jumbo size EGGS (or 4 regular size)
20 RITZ CRACKERS (2/3 cup)	1/2 cup BREAD CRUMBS
1/3 cup BARBECUE SAUCE	1/3 cup HEINZ 57 SAUCE
1/3 cup A1 SAUCE	1/4 cup KETCHUP
1/8 cup MUSTARD	1/4 cup MILK
1/2 cup APPLE JUICE (secret ingredient)	
1/2 cup BACOS CHIPS	1 tsp. SALT
pkg. of frozen VEGETABLES	pkg. of TEXAS TOAST
6 nice IDAHO BAKING POTATOES	
your favorite BAKED POTATO TOPPINGS	

The Home & Garden Party's Bowl and Pitcher set, coffee mugs, place settings, platter, casserole and pizza stone.

These directions are written for the guy that is making a real treat for the family or when it is his turn to cook for the guys. Put the pizza stone on the lower shelf of the oven and preheat the oven to 375°.

Dump the meat into the bowl and make a big hollow place in the middle of the meat. Hand crush the crackers and then add all of the ingredients to the hollow place in the meat. Yes, you are supposed to break the eggs and throw away the shells. Stir the ingredients in the center and then start pulling the meat in as you stir. The meat should be covered with the sauces, but don't over stir or the thing will become pasty when it is cooked.

Use a fork to smooth the top into a dome. Wipe the bowl edge with a paper towel so it will look great after it cooks. Sprinkle the Bacos chips on the top for a crunchy topping. Write your initials on the top with more ketchup.

Wash up the potatoes and place them on the pizza stone that is on the lower shelf. Place the meat loaf on the higher oven shelf. Bake at 375 for 75 to 90 minutes or until the meat thermometer says its done.

Chill or heat the pitcher and mugs, then add your favorite cold or hot drink. Place the vegetables in the casserole and follow the package directions. You can add a can of your favorite cream soup and top it with potato chips. Also, follow the package directions for the Texas Toast and use the platter for them. If you feel really daring, toss a salad, too.

This great meal will serve 12 large helpings or 4 hungry men. Make them guess what your secret ingredients are.

Home & Garden Party
Bean Pot Pizza

Submitted by Nancy Westbay, OH

1 1/2 pounds GROUND CHUCK   small ONION - chopped
16 oz. box ROTINI, (spiral macaroni)   2 - 16 oz cans PIZZA SAUCE
2 - 8 oz. pkgs. MOZZARELLA SHREDDED CHEESE
small can MUSHROOM STEMS and PIECES
3 oz. pkg. PEPPERONI

Brown ground chuck and onion together. Drain, and combine with cooked macaroni, mushrooms and pizza sauce.

Prepare your Home & Garden Party Bean Pot with a vegetable oil spray and then layer ingredients as follows:

Approximately 1/3 of the Macaroni and beef mixture, then 1/3 of the sliced pepperoni, and 1/3 of the shredded cheese. Repeat the layers, ending with a layer of pepperoni, and reserving about 1/3 of the shredded cheese. Cover with lid, place in oven and bake for 1 hour at 325 degrees. After baking, remove from oven and top with reserved cheese. Cover with lid and let it set until the cheese is melted.

Serve with salad and garlic bread.

El Dorado Casserole

Submitted by Carolyn Wilson, CA

Pre-heat oven to 350 degrees

Sauce:

In large skillet brown 1 1/2 to 2 lb. GROUND BEEF and 1 CHOPPED ONION (drain).

Add:

1 large can chopped TOMATOES
1 pkg. CHILI-0-MIX
1 can small OLIVES - drained
1 large can TOMATO SAUCE

Simmer all the above ingredients for 20 minutes.

Mix together in a bowl:

1 pint SOUR CREAM
1 pint COTTAGE CHEESE
1 can chopped GREEN CHILIES

Set aside in two separate bowls:

1 lb grated MONTEREY JACK CHEESE
1 package TORTILLA CHIPS, crushed

In 9x13 baker layer crushed chips, cottage cheese mixture, and sauce. Keep layering chips, cottage cheese mixture, and sauce ending with sauce. Sprinkle chips and grated Monterey Jack Cheese on top. Bake uncovered for 35 to 45 minutes.

Chow Fon Egg Noodles

Submitted by Jeanne Atkins, CA

3 PORK STEAKS (chopped into small pieces)
1 bunch of GREEN ONIONS (chopped)
2 lbs. of BEAN SPROUTS
2 EGGS (scrambled)
SALT & PEPPER
SOY SAUCE
1 pkg. EGG NOODLES (cooked)
dash (AJI-NO-MOTO)

Fry pork steaks until almost done, and then add 1/2 bunch of green onions. While cooking, wash bean spouts, and add to pork steak and green onions. Add scrambled eggs to the pork steak, and ingredients. Add salt, pepper, and soy sauce. Add cooked egg noodles into the mixture, and a dash of Aji-no-Moto, and mix well.
Sprinkle rest of green onions over top.

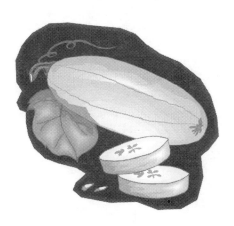

Chicken 'N Biscuit Bake

Submitted by Sharon Siebert, IL

1 can (10-3/4 oz) condensed CREAM OF MUSHROOM SOUP
1 1/2 cups frozen MIXED VEGETABLES
1 cup MILK   3/4 cup ONION, chopped
2 cloves GARLIC, pressed   3/4 cup CELERY, chopped
2 cups chopped, cooked CHICKEN or 2 cans (1 -10 oz. and
     1-5 oz. CHUNK WHITE CHICKEN, drained, and flaked
3 packages (7.5 oz. each) BUTTERMILK BISCUITS
1 1/2 cups (6 oz) shredded CHEDDAR CHEESE

Preheat oven to 350°F. Combine -soup, milk, and garlic in Batter Bowl.
Add chicken and mixed vegetables to soup mixture; set aside.
Add chopped onion and celery to soup mixture, and mix well.
Separate each package of biscuits into 10 pieces. Snip each biscuit into
fourths and add to soup mixture. Stir gently to combine.
Pour mixture into 9x13" Baker. Sprinkle with cheese.
Bake 25-30 minutes or until lightly browned and biscuits are cooked
through. Let stand 5 minutes before serving.

Thick Cheesy Pizza

Submitted by Lynn Pacas, CO

1/4 cup GREEN PEPPER   1/4 cup ONION
1/4 cup BLACK OLIVES   A clove of GARLIC
1 jar SPAGHETTI SAUCE (your choice of what kind and flavor)
3 packages of refrigerated BISCUITS
2 cups grated MOZZARELLA CHEESE

Preheat oven to 375 degrees.
Chop pepper and onion. Slice olive or buy already sliced.
Combine veggies and spaghetti sauce. Press in garlic clove. Mix well
Cut biscuits into quarters arrange half on bottom of 9x13 baker, spread
with sauce mix. Sprinkle with some mozzarella cheese. (Other cheeses
can be added; it's your choice). Repeat layers. Bake for 25 to 30 minutes
or until golden brown. Servings: 8 or so!

Taco Dip

Submitted by Christine Vincent, OH

1 package TACO SEASONING
1 16 oz. container SOUR CREAM
1 8 oz. CREAM CHEESE

With cream cheese at room temperature, place all ingredients in a mixing
bowl. Whip with mixer until smooth. Put on bottom of plate.
Cover with:

shredded LETTUCE   shredded CHEDDAR CHEESE
TOMATO chunks   BLACK OLIVE slices
jalapeno pepper slices (optional)   GREEN ONION pieces (optional)

I always double this, it's enough for 6-8 people. Taste great!!!!!!

Deep Dish Pizza

Submitted by Beth Wilson, ME

About 30 - 40 minutes start to serve.
2 pop-out-of-the-can type BISCUITS - do not use Grands
2 pounds GROUND BEEF
1 small jar PIZZA SAUCE (about 15 ounce)
12 ounces of PIZZA CHEESE

Preheat oven to 350 degrees.
Brown and drain the ground beef.
Flatten out the biscuits and cover the bottom and the sides of the 9 x 13 Stoneware Baker. Tiny spaces may form between the biscuits so just push the biscuits back together.
Combine the ground beef and the pizza sauce. Put this mixture into the biscuit-lined Baker. Cover with a layer of pizza cheese. Bake for 15 minutes. Let stand about 10 minutes to ease cutting. Cut, serve and enjoy.
This will feed 4 to 8 people, depending on the size of each serving.
Pepperoni, green peppers, onions, sausage, etc. may also be added to the ground beef for variety.

Confetti Spaghetti

Submitted by Gloria Alexander, KY

1 package (12 oz.) SPAGHETTI	1-1/2 pounds GROUND BEEF
1 med. GREEN PEPPER, chopped	1 med. ONION, chopped

1 can (14 1/2 oz.) diced TOMATOES, undrained

1 can (8 oz.) TOMATO SAUCE	1 tablespoon BROWN SUGAR
1 teaspoon SALT	1 teaspoon CHILI POWDER
1/2 teaspoon PEPPER	1/4 teaspoon GARLIC POWDER

1/8 teaspoon CAYENNE PEPPER
3/4 cup shredded CHEDDAR CHEESE

1. Cook spaghetti according to package directions; drain.
2. In a large skillet, cook beef, green pepper and onion over medium heat until meat is no longer pink; drain. Stir in the tomatoes, tomato sauce, brown sugar, salt, chili powder, pepper, garlic powder and cayenne. Add spaghetti to the beef mixture.
3. Transfer to Home & Garden Party's 13 x 9 Baker. Cover and bake at 350° for 30 minutes.
4. Uncover, sprinkle with cheese longer or until cheese is m servings

Pizza Pie

Submitted by Claire Doyle, CO
1 can of 8 CRESCENT ROLLS
1 1/2 lbs. BULK SAUSAGE or GROUND TURKEY with spices
1 1/2 cups shredded MOZZARELLA CHEESE
PARMESAN CHEESE sprinkled on top
1/4 cup KETCHUP
1 teaspoon ITALIAN SEASONING
1/2 teaspoon OREGANO
Optional: any toppings you like on pizza such as fresh or drained canned mushrooms, chopped green pepper, red pepper, red onion, green onions, black olives, etc.

Separate rolls and form pie crust in the pie plate bakeware.
Brown and drain sausage or turkey. Add most of mozzarella cheese, add optional veggies, catsup and herbs. Spoon into pie shell, top with remaining cheese. Sprinkle with parmesan cheese. Bake 30-35 minutes at 325°. Let sit 5 minutes before cutting. Could also be baked in the chip and dip pottery if you wanted to double the ingredients for a larger size. Make sure you cook longer though.

Homestyle Pizza

Submitted by Dana McIntyre, NY
(to use with round baking stone)

Preheat oven to 350 degrees.

1 loaf frozen BREAD DOUGH (thawed and risen)
1 lg. can HUNTS TOMATO SAUCE
3 tbsp. OREGANO
1 small can TOMATO PASTE
1/2 c. PARMESAN CHEESE (grated)
1 c. MUENSTER CHEESE (grated)
1 c. MOZZARELLA CHEESE (grated)
1/8 tsp. ROSEMARY
1/8 tsp. PEPPER
1 tbsp. & 1/4 tsp. OLIVE OIL

In food processor mix sauce, tomato paste, oregano, pepper and 1 Tbsp. olive oil. Mix till blended well.

Place risen loaf of dough on round stone and roll out to edges (note: do not over-roll to keep the crust thick and bubbly). Rub 1/4 tsp. olive oil into dough and press rosemary into crust. Sprinkle parmesan cheese all over dough and press in. Spread on sauce and top with mozzarella and muenster cheeses. Add your favorite toppings and bake at 350° for 20-25 minutes!

Cakes

Apple Pizza

Submitted by Michele Ault, OH

2 c FLOUR	1/4 c cold WATER
1/2 c OIL	1 tablespoon SUGAR

Mix and pat evenly onto Home & Garden Party Pizza Stone.
Peel and slice 5 -6 medium apples and place on top of crust.

1 stick OLEO	1/2 c white SUGAR
3/4 c FLOUR	1/2 c brown SUGAR
1 tsp CINNAMON	1/2 c chopped NUTS

Mix topping ingredients and crumble on top of apples.
Bake at 375 for 45 minutes.

Peach Cheese Cream Cake

Submitted by Barb Bowsher, OH

3/4 c FLOUR
1 teaspoon BAKING POWDER
1/2 teaspoon SALT
1 small box of VANILLA PUDDING MIX (not instant)
3 tablespoons BUTTER
1 EGG
1/2 c MILK

Combine above ingredients and beat for 2 minutes, pour into
Home & Garden Party's Pie Plate
1 small can sliced peaches (drained)
Arrange peaches on top of mixture in pan

8 oz CREAM CHEESE	1/2 c SUGAR

3 tablespoons JUICE FROM PEACHES
Beat the above ingredients until smooth and put on top of the
peaches, keeping about 1" from the sides of the pan.
Sprinkle top with sugar and cinnamon and bake at 350 for 30
minutes.

Orange Juice "Yummy" Balls

Submitted by Sheila Tellez, AZ

1 - 12 oz. pkg. VANILLA WAFERS
1 box powdered SUGAR
1/4 lb. MARGARINE, melted
1 (6 oz.) can FROZEN ORANGE JUICE
1 c PECANS, chopped
1 can ANGEL FLAKE COCONUT

Mix together crushed vanilla wafers, powered sugar, margarine,
orange juice and pecans. Make walnut sized balls and roll them
in coconut. Refrigerate. Makes 5 dozens cookies.

Blackberry Cake

Submitted by Carolyn Myers, OH

1 box (18 1/2 oz.) WHITE CAKE MIX WITH PUDDING
1 pkg. (3 ozs.) BLACK RASPBERRY-FLAVORED GELATIN
1 c VEGETABLE OIL   1/2 c MILK
1 c fresh or frozen BLACKBERRIES   4 EGGS
1 c FLAKED COCONUT   1 c chopped PECANS

Icing:

1/2 c BUTTER or MARGARINE, softened
1 lb. CONFECTIONERS SUGAR   4 to 5 tablespoons MILK
1/2 c flaked COCONUT   1/2 c chopped PECANS
1/2 c. fresh or frozen BLACKBERRIES, crushed

In a mixing bowl, combine cake mix, gelatin, oil and milk; mix until blended. Add eggs, one at a time, beating well after each addition. Fold in the blackberries, coconut and pecans. Pour into three greased 9 in. round baking pans. Bake at 350° for 25-30 minutes or until cake tests done; cool in pans 10 minutes before removing to wire racks. For icing, cream butter in a mixing bowl. Add sugar and milk; beat until desired consistency is reached. Stir in blackberries, coconut and pecans. Frost tops of two layers; stack on serving plate with plain layer on top. Frost top and sides of cake. Yield: 12-16 servings.

Home & Garden Party Cake

Submitted by Mary Lee Carson, FL

1 c of THINKING	2 c of DREAMS AND GOALS
3 c of PERSISTENCE	3 teaspoons of ABILITY
1 c of MOTIVATION	5 c of a GOOD ATTITUDE

1 c of RALLIES AND TEAM MEETINGS

Cream together the thinking and the dreams: pour into Home & Garden Party's Pottery and stir until smooth. Sift persistence and ability together and add the motivation to rallies and meetings. Cook well with a good attitude!!!

Temperature: Plenty hot.

Servings will last a lifetime for you and your family!!!! Of course, you may double the recipe!!!!!!

Dirt Cake

Submitted by Dana McIntyre, NY

(to be used with the flower pot and magnolia stem)

1-1/2 lbs. OREO COOKIES	3/4 stick BUTTER (softened)
8 oz. pkg. CREAM CHEESE	1/3 c CONFECTIONERS SUGAR
4 c MILK	GUMMY WORMS (optional)

2 small (4 oz.) pkgs INSTANT VANILLA PUDDING

12 oz. tub FROZEN WHIPPED TOPPING

Crush Oreos in food processor. Mix whipped topping, milk and pudding until thick in medium bowl. In another bowl, combine the cream cheese, butter and sugar. Blend cream cheese mixture with pudding mixture.

Alternately layer the pudding mixture with the Oreos, being sure to end with Oreos on top for "dirt". Garnish with magnolia stem and gummy worms. Great for kids parties.

Lemon Pudding Cake

Submitted by Linda Jenkins-Schneider, OH

Most important item: Home & Garden Party's Hostess Chip & Dipper Plate

1 box YELLOW CAKE MIX	**3/4 c OIL**
1 box LEMON INSTANT PUDDING	**3/4 c WATER**
4 EGGS	

Combine all ingredients and beat at high speed for 5 minutes. Spray Home & Garden Party Hostess Plate. Pour batter into plate. It will be quite full. Don't worry. It is really okay.

Bake 350 degrees for 35-40 minutes. Be sure toothpick or knife comes out of center clean. Cool slightly. About 10 minutes. Carefully pierce entire cake top with fork.

Glaze:
2 c sifted POWDERED SUGAR
1/3 c ORANGE JUICE
2 teaspoons WATER
3 tablespoons melted BUTTER

Mix completely. Using a spatula to spread, slowly pour glaze over warm cake until completely absorbed.

Earthquake Cake

Submitted by Catherine Alton, CA

1 c. PECANS, walnuts or your favorite nuts-chopped
1 c. shredded COCONUT
1 box GERMAN CHOCOLATE CAKE MIX
1 to 2 c. POWDERED SUGAR, according to your sweet tooth
8 oz. CREAM CHEESE
1 stick BUTTER or MARGARINE

Heat oven to 350 degrees. Pam the chip & dip, and then sprinkle nuts and coconut in bottom. Prepare cake mix according to the directions on package and pour into Chipper. Put sugar, cream cheese and butter into the 10" mixing bowl. Heat in microwave until soupy and pour throughout the cake mix. Bake for 35 to 45 minutes, until center is done. Cake will crack as it bakes, hence the name: to serve, cut pieces and flip over onto plate so nuts coconut are on top. Serves 8 to 12.

Mississippi Mud Cake

Submitted by Treva Castleberry, TN

Many different desserts go by the name Mississippi Mud Cake or
Mississippi Mud Pie. Many involve ice cream. Some incorporate
marshmallow, and all include chocolate. This version comes from
the marshmallow camp. It's exceedingly rich and is bound to be
a favorite with everyone you serve it to. Be sure you let the cake
cool before cutting, or it will be too gooey to manage.

4 EGGS, beaten, at room temperature
2 c SUGAR
1-1/2 c FLOUR
1/3 c UNSWEETENED COCOA
6-1/2 ozs. MINI-MARSHMALLOWS

1 teaspoon VANILLA
1 c BUTTER
1-1/2 c chopped PECANS

Frosting:
1/2 c melted BUTTER
3 tablespoons UNSWEETENED COCOA
1 pound POWDERED SUGAR (4 c)

1/3 c MILK
1 teaspoon VANILLA

Preheat oven to 350 degrees. Grease, or line with parchment paper,
a 9x13 pan. In a mixing bowl, beat eggs, sugar, and vanilla. Stir
in flour. In a large saucepan, melt butter; stir in cocoa. Add to egg
mixture; beat well. Pour batter into prepared pan; bake 25 to 30
minutes.

Frosting: Combine butter, milk, and cocoa. Beat in powdered
sugar and vanilla; mix until well combined. When you remove
the cake from the oven, scatter marshmallows all over it. Return
cake to oven briefly to melt marshmallows. Remove cake from
oven and pour frosting over.

Serendipity

Submitted by Dianna Porterfield, OH

1 YELLOW CAKE MIX
1 - 12 oz. bag of CHOCOLATE CHIPS
1/2 bag of MINI MARSHMALLOWS
2 EGGS
1/2 c of OIL
2 tablespoons of WATER

Mix all of the above ingredients together. Grease and flour (or use a spray) your Chip and Dip dish. Pour the mixture in. Bake at 350 degrees for approximately 20-25 minutes. You may want to put something in the bottom of your oven to catch any overspills from the marshmallows,
This is a quick and easy dessert to take anywhere.

Bugs Bunny Cake
(carrot-walnut cake)

Submitted by Connie Ashcroft, NY

4 EGGS
2 c white SUGAR
Beat together.
1 1/2 c CRISCO OIL—add to above

Add:
2 c grated CARROTS
1 c chopped WALNUTS
1 small can drained, CRUSHED PINEAPPLE (approx 8.5 oz can)

Then add:
2 c FLOUR
1 tsp CINNAMON
1 tsp BAKING SODA
1 tsp SALT
Blend well and bake in #99176 9x13 Baker 35-40 minutes.

Icing:
1 large CREAM CHEESE-soft
1 stick MARGARINE or BUTTER-soft
1 lb. CONFECTIONERS' SUGAR
1 tsp VANILLA
Beat together well- it will be like whipped cream
This is just delicious!

Chocolate Mayonnaise Cake

Submitted by Claire Doyle, CO

1 c SALAD DRESSING	2 c FLOUR
2 teaspoons BAKING SODA	2 c SUGAR
3 tablespoons COCOA	2 EGGS
1/2 c cold WATER	1 teaspoon VANILLA

Mix all ingredients for one minute by hand. Pour into greased and floured 9x13 Baker. Bake at 350 for about 1/2 hour or until center of cake is springy. Makes a very moist cake. At higher altitudes, make recipe adjustments adding extra flour.

Carrot Cake

Submitted by Carolyn Wilson, CA

2 c FLOUR	2 teaspoons BAKING POWDER
1 1/2 teaspoons BAKING SODA	1 teaspoon SALT
2 teaspoons CINNAMON	2 c granulated SUGAR
1 1/2 c VEGETABLE OIL	4 EGGS
2 C grated CARROTS	1/2 c chopped WALNUTS

1 (8 1/2 oz.) can CRUSHED PINEAPPLE (drained)

1. Sift together flour, baking powder, baking soda, salt, and cinnamon.
2. Add sugar, vegetable oil, eggs, and mix well.
3. Fold in carrots, drained pineapple, and nuts.
4. Turn unto 9x13 13 baker.
5. Bake at 350 degrees for 35 to 40 minutes (or until cake tests done)
6. When completely cool, ice with Cream Cheese Frosting.

CREAM CHEESE FROSTING

1/4 c BUTTER or MARGARINE   1 teaspoon VANILLA
8 oz. package CREAM CHEESE - softened
1 lb box POWDERED SUGAR

1. Cream margarine, cream cheese, and vanilla together.
2. Add powdered sugar and beat well.
3. If too thick add milk until mixture is of spreading consistency.

7 Up Cake

Submitted by Patty Young, TX

1 box LEMON CAKE MIX   1 box VANILLA INSTANT
PUDDING
3/4 c COOKING OIL   4 EGGS
1 can 7 UP

Combine all ingredients in 9x13 baking pan.
Bake at 350° for 20-30 minutes. Test with toothpick. Leave cake
in pan to ice.

Icing:
2 EGGS   1 No. 2 can CRUSHED PINEAPPLE
1 1/2 c SUGAR   1 stick of OLEO
1 c FLAKED COCONUT   2 tbsp. CORN STARCH or FLOUR

Cook everything together and thicken.
Pour on cake when done.

Fresh Apple Pound Cake

Submitted by Patty Young, TX

3 c FLOUR, unsifted	1 tsp. BAKING SODA
1 tsp. SALT	1 1/2 c CORN OIL
2 c SUGAR	3 EGGS
2 tsp. VANILLA	
2 c APPLES, finely chopped and pared	
1 c PECANS, chopped medium fine	

Preheat oven 325°. Grease and flour a large bundt pan. (Home & Garden Party's Mixing Bowl with the lotion dispenser filled with water and centered in bowl to make a bundt pan.)

Mix flour, baking soda and salt. In large bowl, at medium speed, beat together the oil, sugar, eggs and vanilla. Gradually beat in flour mixture until smooth.

Fold in apples and pecans.

Bake approx. 1 hour and 20 minutes. Until cake tester inserted comes out clean.

Allow to cool in pan on wire rack for 20 minutes.

About 5 minutes before the cake has finished cooling, in a small saucepan, stirring constantly, bring the butter, brown sugar and milk to a boil for 2 minutes.

With a small spatula loosen cake edges and around tube. Turn out on rack.

Spoon the hot sugar mixture over the still warm cake, allowing it to run down the sides. Cool completely.

Minty Dirt Cake

Submitted by Beth Parker, IN

1 boxed DEVIL'S FOOD CAKE MIX (any brand, I use Pillsbury)
WATER (follow box directions for amount)
EGGS (follow box directions for amount)
VEGETABLE OIL (follow box directions for amount)
approx. 40 ANDES MINTS (this brand works best)
1 tub CHOCOLATE FROSTING (I use Pillsbury fudge frosting)
approx. 5 or 6 OREO (or any brand chocolate sandwich cookies)

1. Preheat oven per box directions.
2. Mix cake mix, water, oil, and eggs in Home & Garden Party FLOWER POT until smooth and well blended.
3. Cut Andes mints in half and add to cake batter. Mix until evenly dispersed.
4. Clean around top of flower pot to remove any splattered batter (if left it will burn and turn black).
5. Bake in preheated oven for approximately 45 to 60 minutes (takes a little longer since the pottery is thicker than metal pans)
6. Remove from oven and ice, while still warm.
7. Place Oreos in a Ziploc baggie and seal. Crush with a rolling pin or mallet until it looks like "dirt". (They will begin to look like potting soil.) Sprinkle over icing, and press into place.
8. For added effect, place a silk plant in the center of the cake and add gummy worms to the "dirt".
9. ENJOY!

*Note: Cake will be a little "fudgy" in the center. That is ok. It tastes more like brownies. Serve with a spoon, dip it right out of the pot. No need to cut it.

My customers had no idea that I had a cake the first time I made it and took it to a show.

Better Than Anything Chocolate Cake

Submitted by Alisha E. Glenn, WI

CHIP & DIPPER
1 pkg. CHOCOLATE CAKE
1 jar MRS. RICHARDSON CARAMEL FUDGE
1 4 oz. can CONDENSED MILK
8 oz. SEMI-SWEET MILK CHOCOLATE CHIPS
8 oz. COOL WHIP

Make cake according to directions on pkg. Pour 3/4 of batter into Chip & Dipper and bake for 15-18 min.

Pour 3/4 caramel fudge over cake. Sprinkle 3/4 chocolate morsels over. Pour remainder of cake batter. Bake 12-15 minutes longer. Remove from oven let cool for 15-20 min. Sprinkle remainder of chocolate morsels. Pour over remainder of caramel fudge. Cover with cool whip and serve!!

Blueberry Cheese Cake

Submitted by Eddie Compton, AZ

2 c SIFTED FLOUR	1/2 c BROWN SUGAR
1 c MARGARINE	1 c CHOPPED NUTS

Mix well and press into Home & Garden Party's 13 inch chip & dip. Bake 10-15 minutes in 425 degree oven. Remove and crumble.

Mix one 8 oz package cream cheese and add 1 c Powdered sugar. Whip 2 packages dream whip. Add 1/2 C sugar. Mix with cream cheese mixture until smooth. Crumble crust mixture once more then press back into Chip & Dip Bowl. Pour cream mixture over crust then add 2 cans (about 20 oz. each) blueberry pie mix over cream mixture, chill. Can be spooned or sliced into serving dishes. This is an easy and delicious dessert.

Chocolate Pudding Cake

Submitted by Claire Doyle, CO

2 c buttermilk BAKING MIX (Bisquick)
6 tablespoons + 2/3 c unsweetened COCOA POWDER
2 teaspoons VANILLA   2 c SUGAR
1 c MILK   3 1/3 c hot tap WATER

Heat oven to 350°. In a greased 9x13 baker mix the baking mix, 1 c sugar and the 6 tablespoons of cocoa. Stir in the milk and vanilla until blended. Sprinkle evenly with the remaining 2/3 c of cocoa and the 1 c of sugar. Pour the water overtop, no need to stir. Bake 40 minutes or until top is firm. Dust lightly with confectioners sugar. Spoon while hot into dessert bowls; top cake with sauce and cream, whipped topping or ice cream. At higher altitudes, make necessary adjustments by adding flour.

Triple Treat Torte

Submitted by Theresa Swenson, WI

1/2 c cold BUTTER OR MARGARINE
1 c ALL-PURPOSE FLOUR
2/3 c finely chopped dry roasted PEANUTS
FILLING:
1 c CONFECTIONERS SUGAR
1 package (8 oz.) CREAM CHEESE, softened
1/2 c creamy PEANUT BUTTER
1 carton (8 oz.) frozen WHIPPED TOPPING, thawed. divided
TOPPING:
1 package (3.9 oz.) INSTANT CHOCOLATE PUDDING MIX
1 package (3.4 oz.) INSTANT VANILLA PUDDING MIX
2-3/4 c. cold MILK
grated SEMI SWEET CHOCOLATE, optional

Cut butter into flour until crumbly; stir in the peanuts. Press onto the bottom of a greased 9x13x2" baking dish. Bake at 350 degrees for 16-20 minutes or until golden brown. Cool completely. For filling, beat sugar, cream cheese and peanut butter in a mixing bowl until smooth. Fold in 1 c whipped topping. Spread over crust. In another mixing bowl, combine pudding mix and milk; beat on low speed for 2 minutes. Spread over filling. Top with remaining whipped topping. Sprinkle with chocolate if desired. Cover and refrigerate 4 hours or overnight. Yield: 20-24 servings.

Dirt Cake

Submitted by Susan Janezich, MN

1 pkg. OREO COOKIES (crushed)	1 c. POWDERED SUGAR
1/2 stick of MARGARINE	8 oz. CREAM CHEESE
3 1/2 c. MILK	13 oz. COOL WHIP
2 small pkg. INSTANT FRENCH VANILLA PUDDING	

Cream margarine, cream cheese and powdered sugar. Use our mixing bowl - put 3 1/2 milk & add instant pudding (beat till thick). Add cool whip & mix with cheese mixture. Use our flower pot to layer this dessert. Layer with crushed oreo and then cream mixture; continue and end with crushed oreo. Add some gummy worms and use a stem from our floral swags. This make for a great gift for around $20.00.

Super Easy Butterscotch Cake

Submitted by Ruth Gangluff, OH

Preheat oven to 350 degrees

Spray 9x13 Bakeware Baker with oil or product such as Pam

Mix together:

1 regular size box of YELLOW CAKE MIX
2 EGGS
1 can BUTTERSCOTCH PUDDING - 15 oz.

Spread evenly in the prepared baking pan.

Mix together:

1/2 c of BROWN SUGAR   **1 c of chopped PECANS**
1 c of BUTTERSCOTCH CHIPS

Sprinkle mixture evenly over batter. Bake for 35 minutes (or tests done).

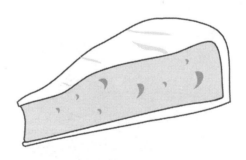

Pig Pickin Cake

Submitted by Kathleen Jones, AZ

Preheat oven 350 degrees
1 box WHITE or YELLOW CAKE MIX
4 EGGS
1 c of OIL
1 can of MANDARIN ORANGES with juice

Beat for two minutes. Bake for appox 1 hr. 15 minutes in 9x13 baker. Remove from oven and cool thoroughly.

FROSTING
1 can of CRUSHED PINEAPPLE
1 package of VANILLA INSTANT PUDDING
Mix together. Fold in one container of whipped topping. Spread evenly on top. Refrigerate for 1/2 hr.

Pumpkin Pie Cake

Submitted by Billie Caffo, PA

Crust:

1 YELLOW CAKE MIX (reserve 1 cup)   1 EGG
1/2 c. melted BUTTER

Filling:

15 oz. PUMPKIN	**1 c BROWN SUGAR**
2/3 c. MILK	**3 EGGS**
1/4 c. SUGAR	**1/2 t. PUMPKIN PIE SPICE**
1/2 t. CINNAMON	

Topping:

1c. RESERVE CAKE MIX	**1/2 c. SUGAR**
1/4 c. melted BUTTER	**1/2 chopped NUTS (optional)**

Combine crust ingredients and press into the 9x13 baker mix filling, pour over crust, crumble topping over filling. Bake at 350° degrees for 50-60 minutes.

Dirt Cake

Submitted by Carolyn Wilson, CA

Crush one 1 1/2 lb. package OREO Cookies and set aside

Cream together:

1/2 stick MARGARINE - softened   8 oz. CREAM CHEESE - softened
1 c POWERED SUGAR

Mix together in separate bowl:

3 1/2 c cold MILK   12 oz. COOL WHIP
1 large package FRENCH VANILLA INSTANT PUDDING

Add cream mixture to pudding mixture and mix well.
In our Pottery Flower Pot layer the crushed cookies and pudding mixture ending with crushed cookies.
Add some artificial flowers and it looks just like a potted plant.

Sour Cream Coffee Cake

Submitted by Carolyn Wilson, CA

Preheat oven to 350 degrees.
Cream Together:
1/2 lb. MARGARINE or BUTTER softened
1 1/4 c SUGAR
Add:
2 EGGS
1 c SOUR CREAM
1 teaspoon VANILLA
Combine:
2 c FLOUR
1/2 teaspoon BAKING POWDER
1/2 teaspoon BAKING SODA
Add gradually to cream mixture.

Place 1/2 of the batter into buttered 9x13 baker and sprinkle on
1/2 of the following topping mixture:
1/2 c granulated SUGAR
1 1/2 teaspoon CINNAMON
4 Tablespoons BROWN SUGAR
1 c chopped PECANS or WALNUTS

Add remaining batter and top with remaining topping.
Bake at 350 degrees 35 to 45 minutes (or until cake tests done)

Cake In a Home & Garden Party Coffee Mug

Submitted by Donna Mossman, TX

1 CAKE MIX - any flavor
1 (4 serving size) INSTANT PUDDING MIX,
    any flavor not sugar free
    Good combinations of flavors are:
    Lemon Cake Mix - Lemon Pudding,
    Yellow Cake Mix - Chocolate Pudding (excellent)
    Devil's Food Cake Mix - Chocolate Pudding
    Pineapple Cake Mix - Coconut Cream Pudding
    Butterscotch Cake Mix - Butterscotch Pudding

Glaze Mix:

1/3 c POWDERED SUGAR
1-1/2 teaspoons DRY FLAVORING
    *Dry flavoring - choose one of the following:
    powdered lemonade mix (not sugar free);
    powdered orange breakfast drink; OR cocoa powder.
    Select the flavoring appropriate to the cake you are making.

Place dry cake mix and dry pudding mix into a large bowl and blend well with a whisk. This will be about 4 to 4-1/2 c dry mix and will make 8 to 9 Coffee Mug Cake mixes.

Place 1/2 cup dry mix into a sandwich bag. Place mix into a corner of the bag and tie it there with a twist-tie. Continue making packets until all your dry mix is used.

Use "Glaze" mix for the flavor of the cake mix you have chosen. Place glaze ingredients into a sandwich bag and tie into corner of bag. Label this "Glaze Mix" and attach it to the other bag with a twist-tie or ribbon.

Place one mix into a coffee mug. Wrap with cello wrap and tie with a bow.

Place one cup in basket with several mixes of different flavors - This way the recipient can make several cakes in their mug over a period of time.

Directions: Generously spray inside of coffee mug with cooking spray. Empty contents of large packet into mug. Add 1 egg white, 1 tablespoon of oil, and 1 tablespoon water to dry mix. Mix for 15 seconds (mix in all dry ingredients). Microwave 2 minutes on HIGH. Mix "Glaze Mix" in small container with 1-1/2 teaspoon water. Mix well - When cake is done pour glaze over cake in cup. ENJOY!

Lemon Pudding Cheese Cake

Submitted by Jeanner Atkins, CA

1 (8oz.) pkg. of CREAM CHEESE
2 c of MILK
1 pkg. of JELLO LEMON INSTANT PUDDING
1 8 in. GRAHAM CRACKER CRUST

Soften cream cheese and blend with 1/2 cup of milk, and set aside. Take the pudding mix and mix it together with the remaining 1 1/2 c of milk. Beat slowly with egg beater just until well mixed; do not overbeat. Mix together the cream cheese mixture and the pudding mixture. Pour on graham cracker crust pie mold, and sprinkle with graham crackers lightly on the top. Let it chill for an hour.

Better Than Anything Cake

Submitted by Gail Burrows, MI

1 box YELLOW CAKE MIX
5-6 large BANANAS
1 can crushed PINEAPPLES (in juice)
1 8 oz. WHIPPED TOPPING
1 c SUGAR
1/2 c COCONUT
1 box INSTANT VANILLA PUDDING (8 servings)
1/2 c chopped NUTS
1 8 oz. CREAM CHEESE (softened)
1 jar MARASCHINO CHERRIES

Using Your 9x13 Home & Garden Party's Party Baker, bake cake mix as directed on box. While cake is baking bring sugar and pineapple with juice to a boil in sauce pan. After you remove cake from the oven, poke holes in the top using the handle of a wooden spoon. Pour pineapple mixture evenly over the holes. Let cake cool completely. Mix pudding as directed on the box. Stir cream cheese into pudding. (May have some small lumps). Spread mixture over cooled cake. Slice bananas and lay across mixture. Spread whipped topping over bananas. Top whipped topping with coconut, nuts and cherries. Chill for 1 to 2 hours. Serve and ENJOY!

Jeannie's Fat-Free & Sugar-Free Punch Bowl Cake

Submitted by Jeannie Zanet, KY

Can be made in the Mixing Bowl or Bean Pot.

One ANGEL FOOD CAKE cut into bite size pieces
One box INSTANT SUGAR-FREE VANILLA PUDDING, mix according
    to directions on box
One small can crushed PINEAPPLE with juice
3 medium BANANAS. sliced
One quart fresh STRAWBERRIES, washed and sliced
One large FAT-FREE COOL WHIP
One small jar of MARACHINO CHERRIES, rinsed

Layer cake on bottom and follow
in order of above, the other
ingredients. Chill!
I take this dessert everywhere!
Even to parties! There is NO
leftovers! It's great!

Gooey Butter Cake

Submitted by Sue Vernier, MI

This is nice to put into the chip and dip.
Butter bottom and sides of chip and dip.
Preheat oven 350°

Mix together:

1 YELLOW CAKE MIX   **1 EGG**
1/2 c melted BUTTER

Mix and press in bottom and up sides of chip dip.

Cream

8 oz. CREAM CHEESE   **2 EGGS**
2 c of POWDERED SUGAR

Spread on top of base mix

Bake for 40-45 min. Do not over bake light brown.
Sift powdered sugar over top while hot.
This is a really yummy cake almost like cheese cake. You can enhance with fruit and sauces or even with different cake mixes. Have done a lot of different flavors with this one. Enjoy!

Wacky Cake -
Easy and rich and NO eggs!

Submitted by Lauretta Kiser, ID

3 cups FLOUR	**2 cups SUGAR**
4 tbps VINEGAR	**4 tbps COCOA**
2 tsp BAKING SODA	**8 tbps. SALAD OIL**
2 cups cold WATER	

Mix and blend in 9x13 Baker. Bake 45 minutes at 350 degrees.

Pies

Grandma's Old Fashioned Cobbler

Submitted by Jeannie Cox, IL

1 stick of BUTTER
1 cup SUGAR
1 EGG
1 large can of sliced PEACHES, drained
   (or any other presweetened fruit)

1 cup self-rising FLOUR
1 cup MILK
1 teaspoon VANILLA

Preheat oven to 350 degrees. Put butter into chip and dip platter and heat in oven until melted. Using a hand whisk, mix together flour, sugar, milk, egg, and vanilla. Pour mixture into chip and dip over hot butter. Drop the peach slices evenly on top, do not stir. Bake for 45 minutes to an hour (or until golden brown).

Easy Fruit Cobbler

Submitted by Treva Castleberry, TN

This recipe has been in my family for years. It is quick, easy and delicious.

4 ounces BUTTER OR MARGARINE, (1 stick)
1 cup SUGAR
1 cup MILK
1 can FRUIT PIE FILLING (cherry, apple, peach etc.)

1 cup FLOUR
1 EGG

Melt butter in 8x8x2 inch pan or pyrex dish. Mix all other ingredients except fruit in separate bowl. Pour this over the butter. Add pie fruit last.
Bake at 350° degrees 45 to 60 minutes or until crust is golden brown.
Serves 8.

Apple Crisp

Submitted by Kim Miller, WI

1 cup ROLLED OATS (quick cook or regular)
1/2 cup FLOUR   **1/2 cup BROWN SUGAR packed**
1/4 tsp SALT   **1 tsp CINNAMON**
1/2 cup (1 stick BUTTER OR MARGARINE)
4 cups peeled and sliced TART APPLES

Preheat oven 350 degrees.

Place apples in pan. Mix ingredients. Put mixture on top of apples.
Bake 30 min- or until top is golden brown

Apple or Peach Pie

Submitted by Martha West, SC

3 cups sliced PEACHES OR APPLES   **1 tbsp. LEMON JUICE**
1 cup self-rising FLOUR   **1 cup SUGAR**
2 EGG WHITES   **5 tbsp. melted MARGARINE**

Place fruit & 12" pie plate. Sprinkle with lemon juice. Mix flour, sugar
and eggs until lumpy. spread over fruit. Pour melted margarine over
top. Bake @ 375 degrees for 30-35 minutes.

Cobbler

Submitted by Cynthia Bower, IL

Melt 1 stick of butter in the 9x13 at 375 degrees. While that is melting, mix 1 c. sugar, 1 c. flour and 1 1/2 tsp. baking powder. Add 3/4 c. milk. Pour over the melted butter. DO NOT STIR TOGETHER. (Batter should start to rise as you are pouring it onto the butter). Spoon 1 large can of pie filling over the batter. Bake at 375 for 35-40 minutes. Best served warm & even better with ice cream on top.
(We like cherry & peach the best.)

Grandma's Special Pumpkin Pie

For the pie plate.
Submitted by Mary Lee Carson, FL

3 cups PUMPKIN	1 cup SUGAR
4 tbs. FLOUR	2 tsp. CINNAMON
1/2 tsp NUTMEG	1/2 tsp GINGER
1 tsp. SALT	1/2 cup dark CORN SYRUP
4 EGGS (beaten)	
3 cups EVAPORATED MILK (undiluted)	

Combine all ingredients and pour into two chilled 9 inch unbaked pie shells that are placed in the Home & Garden Party pie plate bakeware. Bake at 425 for 20 minutes, and then reduce heat to 375 for 20 minutes. Serve with whipped cream... This has been handed down through generations and is a favorite with the whole family!

Granny's Shoofly Pie

Submitted by Carolyn Yonchuk, PA

3 cups FLOUR
1 cup BROWN SUGAR
3/4 cup SHORTENING
2 tsp. BAKING POWDER

1 cup MOLASSES
1 cup boiling WATER
1 tsp BAKING SODA
1 (9") PIE CRUST

Mix flour, brown sugar, shortening and baking powder together to resemble coarse crumbs. Reserve 1/2 cup to sprinkle on top. Mix molasses, water and baking soda, and combine with first mixture. Pour into bottom of unbaked pie shell. Sprinkle with reserved crumbs. Bake at 375° degrees for 30 minutes. Reduce heat to 350° and bake 20 minutes longer. Cool completely before cutting.

Pate Brisee or Pie Crust

Submitted by Sue Vernier, MI

2-1/2 cups all-purpose FLOUR
1 teaspoon SALT   **1 teaspoon SUGAR**
1 cups (2 sticks) cold unsalted BUTTER, cut into small pieces

1. Place the flour, salt, and sugar in a food processor, and process for a few seconds to combine. Add butter. Process until mixture resembles coarse meal, about 8 to 10 seconds. If making by hand, place the dry ingredients in a large bowl. Add the butter, and blend with a pastry cutter until the mixture resembles a coarse meal.
2. Add 1/4 to 1/2 cups of ice water in a slow steady stream through the feed tube of a food processor with the machine running, just until the dough holds together. Do not process the dough for more than 30 seconds. If making by hand, mix the dough with a wooden spoon, adding the water and mixing until the dough just holds together.
3. Turn the dough out onto a piece of plastic wrap. Press the dough into a flatten circle, and wrap it in the plastic. Refrigerate the dough for at least 1 hour. The dough may be double-wrapped in plastic and frozen for several months.

This makes 1 pound, 5 ounces of dough that will make 2 single crusts.

Rocky Road Pie

Submitted by Lori Fischer, CA

one packaged BROWNIE MIX (your choice)
2 cups of MINI MARSHMALLOWS
CHOCOLATE SYRUP OR ICE CREAM TOPPING
CARAMEL SYRUP OR ICE CREAM TOPPING
chopped NUTS (optional)

Mix the brownie mix as directed and pour into the chip and dip platter.
Bake as directed on mix. Let cool. Just before serving, cover with mini
marshmallows and put back in the oven set at 400 degrees. When
marshmallows are lightly toasted, remove from oven and drizzle with
chocolate and caramel. Serve nuts in the dip bowl, for topping.
Variations: Raspberry syrup, chocolate chips instead of syrup.

Lemon Chess Pie

Submitted by Karen Davidson, KY

1 store-bought or homemade PIE CRUST
3 large EGG WHITES
3 large EGGS
1 cup firmly packed LIGHT BROWN SUGAR
1/3 cup LOWFAT MILK
1/4 cup GRANULATED SUGAR
2 tbps LEMON JUICE
1 tbps CORNMEAL
1 tbps ALL-PURPOSE FLOUR
1 tbps BUTTER OR MARGARINE, melted
2 teaspoons grated LEMON RIND
2 teaspoons VANILLA

Preheat oven to 350. Line a Home & Garden Party pie plate with pie crust. Trim crust to 1/2 inch beyond edge of pie plate. Fold under extra crust and crimp edge. Bake for 15 min. Or until light brown. Cool crust for 5 minutes.

Meanwhile, in large bowl, using a rotary beater or fork, beat the egg whites and eggs just until mixed. Whisk in brown sugar, milk, granulated sugar, lemon juice, cornmeal, flour, butter, lemon rind, and vanilla. Pour into crust. Bake for 40 to 45 minutes or until knife inserted in center comes out clean. If edges are browning too quickly, cover with foil. Cool for 1 hour. Serve or cover and store in refrigerator. Serves 8.

Pecan Maple Pie

Submitted by Kristen Davidson, KY

1 store bought or homemade PIE CRUST
2 large EGG WHITES
1 large EGG
1 cup MAPLE-FLAVORED SYRUP OR PURE MAPLE SYRUP
1/2 cup firmly packed LIGHT BROWN SUGAR
2 tbps ALL-PURPOSE FLOUR
1 tbps BUTTER OR MARGARINE, melted
1 112 teaspoons VANILLA
1/2 cup chopped PECANS

Preheat oven to 350. Line a Home & Garden Party pie plate with pie crust. Trim crust to 1/2 inch beyond edge of pie plate. Fold under extra crust and crimp edge. Bake crust for 15 minutes or until light brown. Cool crust for 5 minutes.

In a large bowl, using a rotary beater or fork, beat the egg whites and egg just until mixed. Whisk in the maple-flavored syrup, brown sugar, flour, butter, and vanilla just until smooth. Stir in the pecans.

Pour the syrup mixture into baked crust. Bake for 40 to 45 minutes or until a knife inserted in the center comes out clean. If the edge of the crust is browning too quickly, cover with foil, cool for 1 hour. Serves 8.

Cheese and Peaches Pie

Submitted by Cathie Cordell, PA

(Made in the pie plate, and will look great in all of our new designs)
3 1/4 oz. VANILLA PUDDING (not instant)

3/4 cup FLOUR	**1 tsp. BAKING POWDER**
1/2 tsp. SALT	**3 T. BUTTER**
1 EGG	**1/2 cup MILK**

Combine above ingredients and beat 2 minutes at medium speed. Pour into greased Home & Garden Party's pie plate.
Arrange 2 cups fresh sliced peaches on top of batter.
Sprinkle a little sugar over the top.

1 pkg. (8 oz.) CREAM CHEESE
1/2 cup SUGAR
3 T MILK

Beat 2 min and spoon to 1 inch of edge of batter
Mix 1 Tbsp. sugar and 1/2 t. cinnamon and sprinkle over cream cheese filling.
Bake at 350 degrees for 30-35 min. Refrigerate.

Peach Cobbler

Submitted by Connie Eck, PA

3 large cans SLICED PEACHES
1/4 cup BROWN SUGAR
1/4 cup BUTTER (margarine)
1 T. CINNAMON
2 cups FLOUR
2 cups SUGAR
1 tsp SALT
2 tsp BAKING POWDER
1 cup OIL
2 EGGS

Drain 2 cans of peaches. Third can use juice. Put peaches and juice in 9x13 baker. Dot with the 1/4 cup butter. Then sprinkle 1/4 cup brown sugar and 1 T. cinnamon on top. Mix flour, sugar, salt, and baking powder. Mix in oil and eggs. Spread batter over top of peaches. Bake at 350 for 50 minutes.

Peanut-Butter Silk Pie

Submitted by Lisa Newell, KY

Total Prop time. 10 minutes plus chilling
Easy, Microwave used

FILLING:

2 Package (8oz.) CREAM CHEESE, softened
2 cup SUGAR
2 cup CREAMY PEANUT BUTTER
2 tablespoon melted BUTTER OR MARGARINE
2 teaspoon VANILLA EXTRACT
2 cup HEAVY CREAM, beaten until stiff
1 box of PILLSBURY PIE CRUSTS

TOPPING:

2 cup semisweet chocolate chips, 6 tablespoons brewed coffee chopped peanuts, for garnish

1. With your Home & Garden Party Chip & Dip Tray, press both packages of crust in and along the rippled edges. Prick bottom and sides with a fork about 20 times. Bake in preheated 450° oven for 9 to 11 minutes until lightly browned.

2. Make filling: beat cream cheese, sugar, peanut butter, butter and vanilla in a Home & Garden Party Mixing Bowl until creamy. Gently fold in half the beaten cream. Then fold in remaining cream until blended. Spread filling in crust; smooth top.

3. Make topping: Combine chocolate chips and coffee in a Home & Garden Party Cereal Bowl. Cover with plastic wrap. Microwave on high 1 1/2 to 2 minutes; stir until smooth. Cool chocolate slightly. Then pour over top of filling and top with chopped peanuts. Refrigerate pie 1 hour until chocolate is firm, then cover loosely and refrigerate overnight. Makes 12 servings.

This recipe is wonderful for you to serve to your customers the night they attend your party. If you don't have a chip & dip tray, then you need to have a Home & Garden Party in your home to find out how to earn one.

This recipe can also be cut in half and made in our beautiful pie plate.

Strawberry/Rhubarb Crumb Pie

Submitted by Sylvia Paquette, MA

FILLING:
1 EGG
1 c. SUGAR
2 tbsp. FLOUR
1 tsp. VANILLA
3 c. FRESH RHUBARB, cut into 1/2" pieces
3 c. FRESH STRAWBERRIES, halved
1 UNBAKED PIE SHELL - In Home & Garden Pie Plate
TOPPING:
3/4 c. FLOUR
1/2 c. packed BROWN SUGAR
1/2 c. quick-cooking OATMEAL
1/2 c. BUTTER OR MARGARINE

In a mixing bowl, beat egg. Beat in sugar, flour and vanilla; mix well. Gently fold in rhubarb and strawberries. Pour into pie shell. For topping, combine flour, brown sugar and oats in a small bowl; cut in butter until crumbly. Sprinkle over fruit.

Bake at 400 degrees for 10 min. Reduce heat to 350 degrees; bake for 35 to 45 minutes or until golden brown and bubbly. SERVE with VANILLA ICE CREAM. YUMMY!!!

Fresh Peach Pie

Submitted by Gwenda Rotz, PA

1 cup SUGAR   3 t. CORNSTARCH
2 cup WATER

Bring to boil and cook about 3 minutes. Add 1 small box peach jello.
Cook to lukewarm. Add (6) six cups fresh peaches. Mix together and
pour into a baked pie shell.
Ready made pie crust works real well in our pie plate. Cool and top
with cool whip.
P.S. Any fresh fruit will do.

Home & Garden Party
Easy Cherry Cobbler

Submitted by Judy Schaff, NV

1 Home & Garden Party Party Chip N Dip
1 Home & Garden Party Party Batter Bowl or Cereal Bowl
1 Home & Garden Party Party Mixing Bowl
BISCUIT TOPPING:
2 cups ALL-PURPOSE BAKING MIX
2 tablespoons plus 2 teaspoons SUGAR, divided
6 tablespoons MILK
4 tablespoons BUTTER OR MARGARINE, melted
2 teaspoons LEMON ZEST
1/4 teaspoon GROUND CINNAMON
FILLING:
2 cans (21 oz. each) CHERRY PIE FILLING
2 cans (approx. 8oz. each) SLICED PEACHES IN JUICES
4 teaspoons LEMON JUICE
1 teaspoon GROUND CINNAMON
VANILLA ICE CREAM (optional)

Preheat oven to 425 degrees.

For biscuit topping, combine baking mix, 2 tablespoons of the sugar, milk, butter and lemon zest in the batter bowl or cereal bowl; stir until mixture forms dough. Combine the remaining 1 teaspoon sugar and cinnamon in a shaker and set aside.

For filling, combine pie filling, peaches, lemon juice and cinnamon in mixing bowl and mix gently. Microwave on high 7 minutes or until hot being sure to stir after 4 minutes. Pour into chip n dip and drop 6 scoops of biscuit topping dough over the hot filling. Sprinkle with the cinnamon-sugar. Bake 18-20 minutes or until topping is golden brown. Can serve hot or cold and with ice cream if desired.

Serves approximately 12. Recipe can be cut in half and baked in the bakeware pie plate for 3-4 minutes, stirring after 2 minutes.

Strawberry Tart

Submitted by *Deana Bennett*, VA

CRUST:
1 cup (2 sticks) BUTTER, melted
2 cups ALL-PURPOSE FLOUR
1 cup PECANS, finely chopped
FILLING:
1 package (8 ounces) CREAM CHEESE, at room temperature
1 cup CONFECTIONERS SUGAR
1 tsp. VANILLA EXTRACT
1 container (12 ounces) WHIPPED TOPPING, thawed
GARNISH:
3 pints fresh STRAWBERRIES, hulled and washed
1 pint BLUEBERRIES, washed
1/2 cup STRAWBERRY JELLY, melted over low heat

1. Crust: Heat oven to 350 degrees. Coat chip and dip platter with nonstick cooking spray.
2. Combine butter, flour and pecans in medium size bowl. Press mixture over bottom of platter.
3. Bake in 350 degrees oven for 20 minutes. Let cool.
4. Filling: With electric mixer on medium speed, beat together cream cheese and confectioners sugar in large bowl until well blended and fluffy, about two minutes. Beat in vanilla. Fold in whipped topping. Spread over cooled crust.
5. Garnish: Place each strawberry, cut side down, on top of filling to cover pie along with blueberries. Brush berries with melted jelly.
Refrigerate until ready to serve.

Misc. Desserts

Strawberry Twinkie Dessert

Submitted by Carolyn Myers, OH

4 cups STRAWBERRIES, sliced
1 (13 1/2 oz.) jar STRAWBERRY GLAZE
8 TWINKIES
1 (8 oz.) pkg. CREAM CHEESE, softened
1 (14 oz.) can SWEETENED CONDENSED MILK
1 (12 oz.) container NONDAIRY WHIPPED TOPPING

Combine strawberries and glaze in a small bowl.
Slice Twinkies in half lengthwise, and place in a single layer over the bottom of a Chip N Dip.
In a mixing bowl, beat cream cheese and condensed milk until smooth. Fold in whipped topping, and spread mixture over Twinkies. Spoon berries over cream cheese mixture. Cover and chill 30 minutes or more. Refrigerate leftovers.

Grandma's Peach Gravy

Submitted by Mary Lee Carson, FL

Stew about 2 cups of peaches and cover with water. (Peaches will make their own sugar). Add 1 tbsp. butter.

Make a thickening of 1 tbsp flour and 1/3 cup half and half. Add to peaches and bring to a boil. Pour in the Home & Garden Party gravy boat. Place two slices of bread on your Home & Garden Party dinner plate, pour gravy over the top and enjoy!!!!!!!

Dave's Autumn Apple Dessert

Submitted by Marlene Cox, PA

This recipe looks great served in our Apple Chip and Dip or in the 9x13 stoneware baker.

5 medium APPLES, pared, cured, and sliced (to make about 5 cups)
1 (14 oz) can of SWEETENED CONDENSED MILK
1 teaspoon GROUND CINNAMON
1/2 cup BUTTER (1 stick) plus 2 more tablespoons (butter must be cold)
1/2 cup firmly packed BROWN SUGAR
1 1/2 cups BISQUICK
1/2 cup CHOPPED NUTS or (best) "heath crunch bits o'brickle" baking chips. (if you can't find these - you can crush enough heath bars to make about 1/2 cup.)

Preheat oven to 325° F. In our Home & Garden Party mixing bowl, combine apples, sweetened condensed milk, and cinnamon. In a large bowl, cut 1/2 cup butter into 1 cup of Bisquick until crumbly. Stir in apple mixture.

Pour into our chip and dip or 9x13 baker. In small bowl, combine remaining 1/2 cup Bisquick and the brown sugar. Cut in remaining 2 T butter until crumbly. Add nuts or Bits O'Brickle or both. Bake 40-50 mins. or until golden. Serve warm with ice cream if desired.

Banana Pudding

Submitted by Fay Smith, VA

3 small pkg. of instant VANILLA PUDDING
8 ounce container COOL WHIP (let thaw)

5 cups of MILK   8 ounce container SOUR CREAM
BANANAS   VANILLA WAFERS

Mix the vanilla pudding and milk together in a Home & Garden Party mixing bowl. Beat for 2 minutes. Mix sour cream and cool whip in another bowl and then fold into pudding. Layer pudding with bananas and vanilla wafers in a Home & Garden Party Bean Pot or the 9x13 Baker. Refrigerate until ready to serve.

Chocolate Monica

Submitted by Dianna Porterfield, OH

BROWNIE MIX   1 large COOL WHIP
2 boxes of INSTANT CHOCOLATE PUDDING
package of CANDY BARS (your choice, I prefer Butterfinger)

Make brownies according to box directions. Make instant pudding according to box directions, except eliminate 1/2 cup of milk per box. Crumble candy bars.
Layer the above in the mixing bowl - brownie, pudding, candy bar, whip cream. Layer as many times as you can, be sure to leave a little of the candy bar to crumble on top.
I originally got the recipe from a friend (Monica Lytle), and she didn't have a name for it, so we named the dessert after her.

Easy Fruit Dessert

Submitted by Kathy Tewes, IA

FIRST LAYER:

In our 9x13 baker place a layer of MINIATURE MARSHMALLOWS

SECOND LAYER:

1 WHITE BOX CAKE MIX- follow directions on box EXCEPT DECREASE the water by 2 Tablespoons. When mixed, pour cake mix over the marshmallows.

THIRD LAYER:

Top the cake mix with your favorite PIE FILLING. Our favorite is blueberry; however, they are all great.

With this recipe you can mix and match. Chocolate cake mix with cherry pie filling or apple cinnamon with yellow cake mix, etc.

You bake it at 350° degrees for about 45 min.

Fruit Pizza

Submitted by Dawne Kline, OH

Crust:

1 1/2 c. FLOUR	1 stick OLEO
5 tbsp. POWDERED SUGAR	

Combine above and pat onto round baking stone or the chip and dip platter. Bake 350 degrees for 10 minutes.

Filling:

8 oz. CREAM CHEESE	1/2 c. POWDERED SUGAR
1 cup COOL WHIP	

Spread on cold crust. Top with fresh fruit (Strawberries, Kiwi, green and red seedless grapes, bananas, blueberries). Sprinkle fresh fruit with surejell - towel dry before placing on filling. May be made the day before.

Apple Pizza

Submitted by Michele Ault, OH

2 c. FLOUR   1/4 c. cold WATER
1 tbsp. GRANULATED SUGAR   1/2 c. OIL

Mix and pat evenly onto a round baking stone or greased chip & dip. Peel and slice 5 medium apples on top of crust.

1 stick MARGARINE   1/2 c. GRANULATED SUGAR
1/2 c. LIGHT BROWN SUGAR   1 tsp. CINNAMON
3/4 c. FLOUR   1/2 c. chopped NUTS (optional)

Mix with bands and crumble on top of apples. Bake at 375° for 25-30 minutes. 12 Servings.

Cherry Crunch

Submitted by Tracy Pavetti, PA

For 12" STONEWARE PIE PLATE
1 pk YELLOW OR WHITE CAKE MIX   1/4 c. chopped NUTS
2 T BROWN SUGAR   2 tsp. CINNAMON
1 21 oz can CHERRY PIE FILLING 1/2 c. melted BUTTER

Mix cake mix, chopped nuts, brown sugar and cinnamon in Home & Garden Party mixing bowl (of course). Empty pie filling into pie plate top with cake mixture - drizzle with melted butter. Microwave 12-14 minutes. Let stand 5 minutes and serve warm w/vanilla ice cream. YUM!!

Grandma's Old-Fashioned Gingerbread With Nutmeg Sauce

Submitted by Ruth Payne, CA

1 c BROWN SUGAR	2 EGGS, well beaten
3/4 c SORGHUM MOLASSES	3/4 c SWEET BUTTER, melted

Mix and set aside.

Sift:

3 c FLOUR	1 tsp GINGER
1 tsp CINNAMON	1 tsp BAKING SODA
1/4 tsp SALT	

Add this mixture alternately with 1 cup of buttermilk to the first mixture. Beat until blended. Do not over beat. Pour into oiled/sprayed/seasoned 9x13 baker. Bake @ 375° for about 30 min or until toothpick is clean.

Nutmeg Sauce

Submitted by Ruth Payne, CA

3 1/2 c. MILK	1/2 cube SWEET BUTTER
1/3 c. SUGAR	1/4 tsp. SALT
1 tsp. NUTMEG	1/3 c. FLOUR

In saucepan add the milk and butter. Let milk get hot, but not boiling on medium heat. Sift together flour, sugar, salt and nutmeg. Mix well and slowly add to hot milk mixture, stirring constantly to keep from lumping, until thick like a gravy.

Keep warm in gravy boat until served.

*note: If Sauce becomes too thick, add a little milk with a beater to make nice and smooth.

Orange Jello Dessert

Submitted by Raelene Decker, PA

1 - 3 oz. box ORANGE JELLO
1 - 3 oz. box TAPIOCA PUDDING
1 - 3 oz. box VANILLA PUDDING
1 - 8 oz. container COOL WHIP
1 - small can crushed PINEAPPLES
2 - cups boiling WATER
2 - small cans MANDARIN ORANGES

Mix jello and pudding with water and bring to a full boil. Let chill. Then add cool whip. Drain some of the juice off of the pineapples and oranges. Add pineapples and "some" of the oranges. Reserve some of the oranges for the top. Place in the Home & Garden Party "BEAN POT" or "COOKIE JAR". Top with remaining oranges.

I have also substituted "raspberry" jello for the orange jello and raspberries for the mandarin oranges, Add some miniature marshmallows, too! You can also double this, and put it in the 9x13 Baker.

Second Only to the Lord

Submitted by Raelene Decker, PA

Crust (Bake in 9x13 Home and Garden Baker)

1 cup plain FLOUR   **1 cup NUTS**
1 stick melted BUTTER

Mix and press in stoneware baker pan. Bake 20 min. at 350 degrees. Cool completely.

First Layer:

8 ounces of CREAM CHEESE   **1 cup POWDERED SUGAR**
9 ounces of COOL WHIP

Soften cream cheese and stir vigorously till fluffy. Beat in powdered sugar. Fold in cool whip till mixed. Spread over crust in casserole.

Second Layer:

2 BANANAS sliced lengthwise, dip in lemon juice.
1 cup CHERRY PIE FILLING

Layer these on top of first layer. Cover with cherry pie filling.

Third Layer:

I box of VANILLA INSTANT PUDDING
2 cups of MILK

Mix pudding with milk till thick and mostly set. Spread over pie filling. Sprinkle top with nuts and chill,

(This recipe will work beautifully with the chip and dipper stoneware as well.) This dessert is a real crowd pleaser!

Red-White-Blue Dessert

Submitted by Peggy Selken, SD

Use the CHIP N DIPPER
1 PILLSBURY REFRIGERATOR PIE CRUST
1 pkg WHITE CHOCOLATE
8 oz. soft CREAM CHEESE
1 small box INSTANT WHITE PUDDING
1 cup of MILK
STRAWBERRIES AND BLUEBERRIES

Bake and cool pie crust. Melt white chocolate and pour on cooled crust. (While this hardens, dip fresh strawberries in remaining melted white chocolate and set aside.

Mix cream cheese, instant white chocolate pudding and milk. Pour over crust.

Topping:
Dab Cool Whip close to the edge of crust. Then add dipped strawberries and then frozen blueberries (thawed and drained) to cover rest of pie.

Chill - beauitful served in our Chip N Dip Booking Gift.

Chilled Banana Pineapple Dessert

Submitted by Karen Vanadestine, CT

1 1/2 c. SALERNO GRAHAM CRACKER CRUMBS
1/3 c. SUGAR
6 tbsp BUTTER, melted
6 large BANANAS, sliced 1/2" thick, (use ripe bananas for sweetness)
2 sm. boxes of INSTANT BANANA CREAM PUDDING MIX
3 c. MILK
8 oz. CREAM CHEESE, softened
12 oz. COOL WHIP
20 oz. can unsweetened, CRUSHED PINEAPPLE, drained

1. Mix together graham cracker crumbs, sugar and melted butter. Pat firmly into the bottom of the Chip and Dip.
2. Place a layer of the banana slices on top of the crust.
3. In a separate bowl, beat together the milk and pudding mix, with an electric mixer, according to package. Place this on top of the banana layer.
4. Place a layer of the drained pineapple on top of the pudding.
5. Finish with a layer of Cool Whip on the top.
6. Chill this dessert for at least 4 hours, covered with plastic wrap.

Chilled Chocolate Cream Dessert

Submitted by Karen Vanadestine, CT

1 1/2 sticks BUTTER	1 1/2 c. FLOUR
1 tsp. VANILLA EXTRACT	8 oz. CREAM CHEESE, softened

1 1/2 c. chopped WALNUTS, (approx.)
16 oz. container of COOL WHIP, (divided in half)
2 sm. boxes of DARK CHOCOLATE PUDDING, (cook/serve kind)

1 c. CONFECTIONERS SUGAR	3 c. MILK

1. Mix together flour, butter and vanilla, until crumbly. Pat firmly in the bottom of the Chip N Dip. Bake at 350° for 12-15 minutes, or until barely golden. COOL by setting on top of a can, to help air circulate. and cool it faster.
2. Mix in a separate bowl, 1/2 of the cool whip, the softened cream cheese and the confectioners sugar. Place this mixture on top the cream cheese layer.
3. Place a layer of the remaining Cool Whip on top of the pudding.
4. Finish with chopped walnuts on top.
5. Chill this dessert, covered with plastic wrap, for at least 4 hours.
6. This dessert can also be made with instant pudding, but is best with the cooked kind.

Banana Split

Submitted by Kathy Cotterman, MN

2 cups GRAHAM CRACKER CRUMBS

1/2 cup BUTTER	2 EGGS
2 cups POWDERED SUGAR	3/4 cup MARGARINE
1 tsp. VANILLA	12 oz. CRUSHED PINEAPPLE
3 cups BANANNA	12 oz. COOL WHIP

Crush graham crackers. Melt and add butter to crackers. Spread on bottom of pan. Beat eggs 4 minutes on high. Add powdered sugar, margarine and vanilla. Spread over crackers.

Drain pineapple, and spread over filling. Lay bananas over pineapple, and cover with Cool Whip. Refrigerate 6 hours.

Chocolate Chunk Pizza

Submitted by Shelley Herrmann, OH

1 cup FLOUR	1/2 tsp. BAKING SODA
1/4 tsp. SALT	6 tbsp. BUTTER
1/3 cup GRANULATED SUGAR	1/3 cup BROWN SUGAR
1 tsp. VANILLA	1 large EGG

5 cups SEMISWEET CHOCOLATE (broken in pieces)

1/2 chopped WALNUTS or PECANS

Preheat oven to 375. In our mixing bowl melt margarine in microwave. With a wisk, stir in sugars vanilla and egg until mixed. With spoon , stir in flour mixture. Stir in chocolate and nuts. Spoon batter onto our chip and dip platter. Bake 20-30 minutes.

This is a great recipe because it is quick and easy to prepare and bake. Great to take to parties to help get bookings for our chip and dip set.

Rhubarb Dessert

Submitted by Kathy Cotterman, MT

BOTTOM LAYER:

1 heaping tablespoon BUTTER   1 tablespoon FLOUR
4 heaping cups of RHUBARB, cut into 1 inch pieces
    or 2 - 15 ounce packages of FROZEN RHUBARB
1/2 cup SUGAR   1/2 package dry RED GELATIN
1 10 1/2 oz bag MINIATURE MARSHMELLOWS

TOP LAYER:

1 cup SUGAR   2 EGGS
1 teaspoon VANILLA   1/2 cup SHORTENING
dash SALT   1 cup MILK
2 cups FLOUR   2 teaspoons BAKING POWDER
Optional WHIPPING TOPPING or CREAM GARNISH

Bottom Layer: Generously butter 13x9 Baker. Sprinkle with flour. Spread the rhubarb in the pan. Sprinkle with all the sugar and dry gelatin. Cover with a layer of marshmallows.

Top Layer: Stir baking powder with flour. Add 1 cup flour alternating with 1/2 cup milk to cream mixture. Beat to smooth. Add remaining flour and milk and beat smooth. Pour batter mixture over rhubarb in pan, spreading over all. Bake in middle rack in 350 degree oven for 35 to 45 minutes until golden brown or batter tests done. Cool.

To serve: Cut into squares. Serve pieces upside down, topped with light cream or garnished with a whipped topping. (Use either raspberry or strawberry gelatin to make this delicious dessert. It is good).

Fruit Cocktail Cake Pudding

Submitted by Jeanne Atkins, CA

1 cup of FLOUR	1 tsp. BAKING SODA
1 cup of SUGAR	1 EGG
2 1/2 cans of FRUIT COCKTAIL	1 cup of NUTS

Beat egg and sugar, sift in flour, and baking soda, and a dash of salt. Mix well. Drain fruit cocktail, add to mixture, then add nuts, and combine. Pour into a 9x13 bakeware dish. Sprinkle lightly with brown sugar. Bake in oven for 1 1/2 hours at 275°.

Baked Pineapple

Submitted by Barb Crespin, OH

1 can CRUSHED PINEAPPLE (no heavy syrup)
1 cup grated LONGHORN CHEESE
1/2 cup SUGAR
2 EGGS (beaten)
2 tbps. CORN STARCH dissolved in 1/2 cup WATER

Mix above ingredients. Pour into casserole dish and bake at 350° for 1 hour.

Apple Raisin Bread Pudding

Submitted by Helen Shoda, IN

4 cups (about 1 1/2 1b) sliced, cored, pared tart APPLES
1 teaspoon NUTMEG
1 tablespoon BUTTER or MARGARINE
1/2 cup seedless RAISINS
2 cups (about 4 slices) small BREAD CUBES
3 cups MILK, scalded
1/2 cup SUGAR
1/4 teaspoon CINNAMON
1/4 teaspoon NUTMEG
1/8 teaspoon SALT
3 EGGS well beaten
3 tablespoons melted BUTTER or MARGARINE
1 teaspoon VANILLA

1. Arrange apple slices on bottom of well buttered in Apple pattern mixing bowl. Sprinkle nutmeg over top of apples, and dot with butter or margarine
2. Combine bread cubes and scalded milk in butter in bowl. Soak bread 10 minutes. Apples may float.
3. Combine raisins, sugar, cinnamon, nutmeg and salt in a separate small bowl; stir in eggs, melted butter or margarine, and vanilla.

Bake at 350° for 1 1/4 hours.

Peppermint Dessert Cheeseball

Submitted by Linda White, VA

1-12 oz. STARLIGHT HARD PEPPERMINT CANDIES
1-8 oz. CREAM CHEESE
1-12 oz. MINI CHOCOLATE CHIPS
NUTS -optional

Thin chocolate wafers (Find these in the ice cream topping section at your store. Other wafers are not the same!)

Blend peppermint candies in blender or food processor. Blend until they become dust.

Then add cream cheese and blend. Then add mini choc. chips. Roll in chopped nuts. Place on a Home & Garden Chip and Dip and form cheeseball in center and around the cheeseball place thin wafers.

You can also use this as a spread. Just mix in nuts and serve in a Home & Garden Party Cereal Bowl or use Chip and Dip. Place spread in the dip bowl and wafers around.

This is different and tastes GREAT!

Strawberry Twinkie Dessert

Submitted by Gloria Alexander, KY

4 cups STRAWBERRIES, sliced
1 (13 1/2 ounce) jar STRAWBERRY GLAZE
8 TWINKIES
1 (8 ounce) package CREAM CHEESE, softened
1 (14 ounce) can SWEETENED CONDENSED MILK
1 (12 ounce) container NON-DAIRY WHIPPED TOPPING

Combine strawberries and glaze in Home & Garden Party Mixing Bowl. Slice Twinkies in half lengthwise, and place in a single layer over the bottom of a Home & Garden Party 9x13 Baker.

In the Home & Garden Party Mixing Bowl, beat together the cream cheese and sweetened condensed milk. Fold in whipped topping and spread mixture over Twinkies. Spoon berries over cream cheese mixture. Cover and chill 30 minutes or more. Refrigerate leftovers.

Banana Creme Supreme

Submitted by Sandy Boeckman, IA

1 PILLSBURY REFRIGERATED SUGAR COOKIE

Bake at 350 degrees for 12 minutes. Remove from oven and set timer for 10 minutes. After 10 minutes run a serrated bread knife under the crust to pop it off the stone so it does not get hard and stick to the stone. (Do not remove from stone.)

8 oz. CREAM CHEESE   **1/3 cup SUGAR**
2 BANANAS   **pint of HALF AND HALF**
3.9 oz. BANANA CREME INSTANT PUDDING
HERSHEY'S CHOCOLATE SYRUP
chopped NUTS

Mix pint of half and half with pudding mix in our mixing bowl and set aside.

Mix sugar and creme cheese together and spread on cooled cookie. Top with sliced bananas.

Spread pudding mix on top of this.

Drizzle with chocolate and top with nuts!

Summer Sherbet Delight

Submitted by Phyinda Odenbach, AZ

2 cups RASPBERRY SHERBET
1 8 oz. container of NON DAIRY TOPPING (like Cool Whip)
1 PRE-BAKED ANGEL FOOD CAKE (from the bakery!),
    break into bit size pieces
1 bag of MIXED BERRIES
    (Strawberry, Raspberry and Blueberry), thawed and
    sweetened with some sugar

Put the stoneware bowl into the freezer for about 15 minutes to get it nice and cold before layering the ingredients.

Mix the raspberry sherbet and non dairy topping together and set aside. Put 1/2 of the broken angel food cake pieces into the bottom of the bowl.

Next layer 1/2 of the sherbet mixture onto the cake. Layer 1/2 of the berries on the sherbet mixture. Then repeat another layer using the remaining ingredients. Put back into the freezer for about 10 minutes to re-set the sherbet. ENJOY, but don't forget that important piece of angel food cake at the end!!!

Variations:
You can also change the sherbet and fruit. Try pineapple sherbet with bananas, pineapple, coconut and kiwi for a tropical dessert or try orange sherbet with mandarin oranges for an orange creamsicle dessert, etc.

Sweet Bread

Monkey Bread

Submitted by Carolyn Myers, OH

1 pkg. (3 1/2 oz.) cook and serve BUTTERSCOTCH PUDDING MIX
3/4 cup SUGAR
1 tablespoon GROUND CINNAMON
1/2 cup finely chopped PECANS, optional
1/2 cup BUTTER or MARGARINE, melted
2 tubes (10 oz. each) refrigerated BISCUITS

In a plastic bowl with tight-fitting lid, combine pudding mix, sugar, cinnamon and pecans if desired. Pour the butter into a shallow bowl. Cut the biscuits into quarters. Dip several pieces into the butter, then place in bowl; cover and shake. Remove to a greased flower pot. Continue until all the biscuit pieces are coated. Bake at 350°° for 30-35 minutes. Cool in pan for 30 minutes before inverting onto a serving plate. Yield: 10-12 servings.

Christmas Banana Bread

Submitted by Debi Bleile, OH

1/2 cup BUTTER
1 1/3 SUGAR
1/4 cup SOUR CREAM
2 EGGS
2 cups FLOUR
1 t. ALMOND EXTRACT
Hand mix.

1 1/2 t. BAKING POWDER
1/2 t. BAKING SODA
1/4 t. SALT
1 cup ripe, mashed, BANANAS
2 T. RUM

Cream butter and sugar until light and fluffy. Beat in eggs and sour cream - set aside. Mix flour, baking soda, baking powder and salt together. Blend into creamed mixture 1/2 at a time. Add mashed bananas and mix well. Add rum and extract. Turn into loaf pan (greased and floured or sprayed). Bake 60-70 minutes at 325° until tested clear.

Strawberry Bread

Submitted by Pat Ingersoll, UT

2 10 oz. packages FROZEN STRAWBERRIES, thawed
4 EGGS
3 cups FLOUR
1 teaspoon SALT
3 teaspoon CINNAMON
1 1/4 cups OIL
2 cups SUGAR
1 teaspoon BAKING SODA
1 cup chopped NUT

Stir thawed strawberries, eggs and oil together. Add flour, sugar, cinnamon, baking soda, salt and nuts. Stir until just blended. Pour into 2 Home and Garden Party Bakeware loaf pans. Bake at 350° for 1 hour or until centers are done. Test with toothpick. Cool and slice, or wrap in foil and store in refrigerator. Spread with cream cheese before serving.

Banana Bread

Submitted by Melissa Weltz, OK

1/3 cup SHORTENING
2/3 cup SUGAR
1 EGG beaten
1 3/4 cup FLOUR
2 tsp. BAKING POWDER
1/2 tsp. BAKING SODA
3 ripe BANANAS

Preheat oven to 350°°. In Home & Garden Party mixing bowl, cream together shortening, sugar and egg. Set aside. In smaller bowl, combine flour, baking powder and soda. In separate bowl, cut bananas into small pieces and mash with a fork. Add bananas to shortening mixture. Stir in flour mixture until well blended. Do not beat with an electric mixer. Batter should be slightly lumpy. Spray Home & Garden Party loaf pan with non-stick cooking spray and pour in batter. Bake for approximately 1 hour or until knife inserted comes out clean.

Pumpkin Bread

Submitted by Claire Doyle, CO

2 cups FLOUR
1/2 teaspoon SALT
1 teaspoon BAKING POWDER
1/2 teaspoon CINNAMON
2 EGGS
1 cup PUMPKIN

1 cup SUGAR
1 teaspoon BAKING SODA
1/4 teaspoon CLOVES
1/2 teaspoon NUTMEG
1/2 cup OIL

Mix eggs, oil and pumpkin. Add dry ingredients. Grease the loaf pan. Pour into loaf pan. Bake at 350° for 1 hour. Makes 1 large loaf. Make sure you add flour and make adjustments for high altitudes.

Date & Nut Loaf

Submitted by Debbie Wolf, PA

2 lbs. DATES (cut into half)
1 cup SUGAR
2 teaspoons BAKING POWDER

2 lbs. ENGLISH WALNUTS
1 cup FLOUR
4 EGGS

Put dates and walnuts into a large bowl. Mix sugar, flour and baking powder. Beat eggs and add to flour mixture. Pour that over dates & walnuts and stir. Put in greased 9x13 pan. Bake 45 to 50 minutes at 350° degrees.

This recipe can easily be made in our baker 9x13 pan. Also a 1/2 recipe can be made and baked in smaller pan.

This is a recipe that has been passed down in the family of a friend (Bard Eisely) and is a great old fashion treat.

Banana Nut Bread

Submitted by Leslie Cohen, VA

To be used in bakeware loaf pan.

1 c. MARGARINE	4 EGGS
2 1/2 C. SUGAR	3 c. all purpose FLOUR
6 Tbsp. BUTTERMILK	1 1/2 tsp. SODA
5 BANANAS	2 tsp. VANILLA
1 c. NUTS (ground or finely chopped)	

Cream butter and sugar. Add milk, eggs, soda and flour. Add vanilla, mashed bananas and nuts. Beat well with mixer. Bake at 350° degrees for 1 hour. Makes 2 loaves.

Delicious Banana Pudding

Submitted by Leslie Cohen, VA

To be prepared and served in stoneware mixing bowl.

1 (5 1/2 oz.) pkg. VANILLA FLAVOR INSTANT PUDDING
      & PIE FILLING   3 c. cold SKIM MILK
2 c. FROZEN WHIPPED TOPPING, thawed
50 VANILLA WAFERS   4 large DOLE BANANAS

Prepare pudding according to package directions using the 3 cups of milk. Fold in half of the whipped topping. Reserve 6 Vanilla wafers and 1 banana; slice remaining bananas. Arrange a layer of wafers on the bottom of the mixing bowl. Spread 1/4 of the pudding over the wafers; top with banana slices. Place wafers around side of bowl. Continue layering wafers, pudding and bananas, ending with pudding. Cover and chill 3 hours or until serving time. Slice remaining banana. Cover dish with remaining whipped topping and then garnish with banana slices and wafers. Serves 8-10.

Simple Monkey Bread

Submitted by *Maria Hauersperger, IN*

Using any of our fabulous baking stones or beautiful stoneware.

1 tube of refrigerator BISCUITS
2 tablespoons SUGAR
1 tablespoon ground CINNAMON

Mix cinnamon and sugar in a small bowl. Tear the biscuits into small pieces and dip in cinnamon and sugar mixture. Bake according to directions on biscuit package, usually ten minutes at 375 degrees. You can 'dress this up' by adding sliced apples, crushed nuts, melted butter and dry butterscotch pudding mix (not instant), increasing cooking time by a few minutes.

Apricot Cream Cheese Danish

Submitted by Kathleen Anderson, IN

2 pkgs. of CRESCENT ROLLS   **1 pkg. of CREAM CHEESE**
2 EGGS (or 1/2 cup of egg beaters)   **1 tsp. VANILLA FLAVORING**
1 small jar (10-12 oz.) of APRICOT ALL FRUIT SPREAD
ICING:
1 cup CONFECTIONERS SUGAR   **1/4 cup MILK**

Preheat oven to 375 degrees. You may use the pizza stone or the Chip & Dip Platter for this recipe.

Open your crescent rolls and separate. Lay the rolls with the short side pointed to the center, and with the longer edge over hanging edge of platter. This should use 1 1/2 pkgs. of crescents. With your fingertip press seams to join.

In a small mixing bowl blend together the eggs, cream cheese, and vanilla with a mixer until smooth. Approx. 4 minutes. Pour on top of crescent rolls, and spread almost to the edge.

Top with the All Fruit. Spoon it over the top of the mixture. Next bring in the outer pointed edges of the crescent rolls to the center. If they do not meet, take some of the extra crescent roll to add to the center.

Bake for 15 minutes. Remove to cool. Mix your icing and drizzle over the top.

Preparation time: 10 minutes   Number of servings: 12
(You may substitute other flavors of the All Fruit.)

Apricot Banana Bread

Submitted by Mary Louise Law, KY

1/3 cup BUTTER or MARGARINE, softened
1 cup mashed, ripe BANANAS (2-3 medium)
2/3 cup SUGAR
2 EGGS
1/4 cup BUTTERMILK
1 1/4 cup ALL-PURPOSE FLOUR
1/2 teaspoon BAKING SODA
1 teaspoon BAKING POWDER
1/2 teaspoon SALT
1/2 cup chopped WALNUTS
1 cup 100% BRAN CEREAL (not flakes)
3/4 cup chopped dried APRICOTS (about 6 oz.)

In a pottery mixing bowl, cream butter and sugar. Add eggs, mix well. Combine bananas and buttermilk. Combine the flour, baking powder, baking soda and salt; add to creamed mixture alternately with bananas mixture. Stir in bran, apricots and nuts.
Pour into loaf pan. Bake at 350° for 55-60 minutes or until bread tests done. Cool 10 minutes before removing from pan to a wire rack. Yield: 1 loaf.

Cinnamon Rolls

Submitted by Roxie Gunderson, WI

1 loaf frozen WHITE BREAD DOUGH
1/4 cup BUTTER softened
1/4 cup SUGAR
2-3 teaspoons CINNAMON
SWEET ICING

Let frozen white bread dough thaw just until it can be rolled out and before it begins to rise. Roll dough into rectangle, 15x9 inches. Spread with 1/4 cup butter. Mix sugar and cinnamon; sprinkle over rectangle. Roll up beginning at wide side, Pinch edge of dough slightly into roll to seal well. Stretch roll to make even. Cut roll into 12 slices. Place in greased 9x13 baker. Let rise until double in size. Bake 25-30 minutes at 375 degrees. While warm, frost rolls with icing.

SWEET ICING:
Mix:
1 1/2 cups CONFECTIONERS SUGAR
1 tablespoon MILK
1/2 teaspoon VANILLA
until smooth

VARIATION:
Cinnamon and Caramel Nut Rolls
Before placing sliced dough in 9x13 baker, melt 1/2 cup butter and pour into baker, sprinkle 1/2 cup brown sugar and 1/2 cup chopped walnuts over melted butter. Place sliced dough in baker and bake as directed. Immediately turn pan upside down on large tray. Let pan remain a minute so caramel/nut mixture drizzles down over rolls.

Strawberry Bread

Submitted by Phylinda Odenbach, AZ

4-5 cups of sliced fresh STRAWBERRIES or
    2 -10 oz. packages of frozen STRAWBERRIES

4 EGGS	1 1/4 cup OIL
3 cups FLOUR	2 cups SUGAR
1 Tablespoon CINNAMON	1 teaspoon BAKING SODA
1 teaspoon SALT	1 cup chopped WALNUTS (optional)

Preheat oven to 350° degrees. Grease and flour 2 loaf pans or one 9x13 baker. In a medium bowl stir together strawberries, eggs and oil. In a large bowl blend together all dry ingredients (also nuts if you are adding them). Stir strawberry mixture into dry mixture.

Pour into loaf pans or 9x13 baker and bake for 1 hour or until a toothpick comes out clean.

This is a very moist and yummy recipe which is like Banana Nut Bread only with strawberries!

Amish Cinnamon Bread

Submitted by Jo Ann Stewart, OH

1 cup of MILK   1 cup of FLOUR
1 cup of SUGAR

Mix into a large Ziploc bag. Leave set on the counter top

Day 1 - Do nothing.

Day 2, 3, 4, 5, - Mash bag twice a day.

Day 6 - Add 1 cup of flour, 1 cup of milk, 1 cup of sugar.

Day 7, 8, 9, - Mash and let air out of bag twice a day.

Day 10 - Pour contents into a large pottery baking bowl. Add 1
  cup of flour, 1 cup of milk, 1 cup of sugar. Mix together.

Measure out (4) - (1) cup starters into a large Ziploc bag. Give
these to your friends. Tomorrow will be day one for them.

Add to remainder in the bowl the following:
1 cup of oil, 1/2 cup of milk, 3 eggs, 1 tsp. of vanilla. Mix well
and set aside.
In another mixing bowl, mix the following ingredients: 2 cups of
flour, 2 tsp. baking soda, 2 tsp. cinnamon (optional) depending
on the pudding), 5.1 oz. box of instant pudding of your choice, 1
cup of sugar, 1/2 tsp.salt. Mix well and set aside.
In a small bowl mix together enough sugar and cinnamon to coat
bottom of the baking stone loaf pan and the top of the bread
mixture. Mix dry mixture into the moist one and mix well (add
nuts if wanted). Spray 2 loaf pans with non-stick cooking spray
and coat the bottom with 1/2 of the cinnamon mixture. Pour batter
into pans and put remaining cinnamon an top. Bake at 325 degrees
for 45 minutes to 1 hour or until toothpick comes out clean.

Cookies

Judy's Grandma's Chocolate Chip Oatmeal Cookies

Submitted by Judy Smith, MI

2 cups (less 2 tsp.) FLOUR	3/4 cup WHITE SUGAR
3/4 cup BROWN SUGAR	2 EGGs
1 tsp. hot WATER	1/2 tsp. BAKING POWDER
1 tsp. BAKING SODA	1/4 tsp. SALT
2 cups OATMEAL	2 cups CHOCOLATE CHIPS
1 tsp. VANILLA	1/4 cup WALNUT PIECES

Home & Garden Party pizza stone and bowl from the bowl and pitcher set.

In the bowl, mix the flower and sugars, and then add the rest of the ingredients. The batter will be thick. Drop the batter by teaspoon onto the pizza stone. Bake at 325 for 12 minutes. Makes 3 dozen great cookies.

Cake Mix Oatmeal Cookies

Submitted by Patty Young, TX

1 (18.25 oz.) pkg. YELLOW CAKE MIX
2 cups quick-cooking OATS, uncooked

1 cup SUGAR	1 cup VEGETABLE OIL
2 large EGGS	1 cup chopped PECANS

1 1/2 teaspoons VANILLA extract

Combine first 3 ingredients in a large bowl. Combine oil and eggs; add to dry ingredients, stirring well. Stir in pecans and vanilla. Drop dough by rounded teaspoonfuls 2 inches apart onto baking stone. Bake at 350° for 12 minutes or until lightly browned. Remove to wire rack to cool. Yield: 5 dozen.

Frosted Brownies

Submitted by Shelly Petrey, KY

Prepare brownies according to box to fit the Home and Garden Party's 9x13 baker.

While brownies are baking prepare frosting ......

1 stick BUTTER	**5-6 tablespoons MILK**
3 1/2 tablespoons COCOA	**1 lb confectioners SUGAR**
1 cup chopped PECANS (optional)	**1 teaspoon VANILLA**
1/2 cup PEANUT BUTTER	

While brownies are hot, spread mixture over top. Allow to cool. This is a family favorite that has easily turned into a tradition for gatherings.

Apple Brownies

Submitted by Claire Doyle, CO

3/4 cup BUTTER	**2 cups BROWN SUGAR**
2 cups FLOUR	**1/2 teaspoon SALT**
1 1/2 cups chopped APPLES	**3/4 cup NUTS (optional)**
2 EGGS	**1 teaspoon VANILLA**
2 teaspoons BAKING POWDER	**1 teaspoon CINNAMON**

Grease the 9x13 baker. Mix all ingredients. Bake at 350° for 1/2 hour. Sprinkle with nuts if desired. Then sprinkle with some sugar. High altitudes, make adjustments to recipe by adding extra flour.

Fudge-Topped Brownies

Submitted by Treva Castleberry, TN

These brownies are very rich and will definitely cause you to lick your fingers (and then go cut yourself another one). The gooey, fudge topping is simply to die for.

1 cup BUTTER, melted	2 cups SUGAR
2 teaspoons VANILLA	2 EGGS, at room temperature
1/2 cup MILK, at room temperature	1 cup FLOUR
2/3 cup COCOA	1 cup chopped WALNUTS

1 (14 ounce) CAN SWEETENED CONDENSED MILK
12 ounces SEMISWEET CHOCOLATE CHIPS

Preheat oven to 350 degrees. Grease a 9x13" pan.

In a large bowl, mix butter, sugar, and 1/2 teaspoon vanilla. Add eggs and milk; mix well. Stir in flour and cocoa: then stir in walnuts. Spread in prepared pan. Bake 40 minutes, until brownies begin to pull away from the sides of the pan.

Heat milk and 1-1/2 teaspoons vanilla in a heavy saucepan. Immediately spread over hot brownies; cool, chill, and cut into bars.

Double Chocolate Crispy Bars

Submitted by Pat Ingersoll, UT

1/2 cup BUTTER or MARGARINE
2 cups tiny MARSHMALLOWS
3/4 cup SUGAR
1 6 ounce bag MILK CHOCOLATE PIECES
2 EGGS
1 cup PEANUT BUTTER (chunky)
1 teaspoon VANILLA
1 1/2 cups CRISP RICE CEREAL
3/4 cup FLOUR
1/4 teaspoon SALT
1/2 cup chopped PECANS
2 tablespoons UNSWEETENED COCOA POWDER
1/4 teaspoon BAKING POWDER

Cream butter or margarine and sugar; beat in eggs and vanilla. Stir together flour, chopped nuts, cocoa, baking powder and 1/4 teaspoon salt. Stir in the egg mixture. Spread in bottom of 9x13 Home and Garden Party Bakeware pan.

Bake in 350 oven for 16 to 20 minutes or until bars test done. Sprinkle marshmallows evenly over top. Bake 3 more minutes. Cool.

In saucepan combine chocolate pieces and peanut butter. Cook and stir over low heat till chocolate is melted. Stir in cereal. Spread over cooled bars. Chill, cut into bars. Keep refrigerated until ready to eat. Loved by everyone, no matter their age.

Easy Chocolate Cookies

Submitted by Kathy Tewes, IA

2 boxes DEVILS FOOD CAKE MIX
2 sticks MARGARINE - softened
4 EGGS
Mix and Chill Overnight

TO MAKE OREOS:
Mix 8 oz. cream cheese and 3 1/2 cup powdered sugar. Make cookie dough in small balls and bake... frost with above mixture and eat.

TO MAKE CARAMEL FILLED COOKIES:
Roll cookie into ball and stick the Rolo in the middle. Make sure the dough covers the entire Rolo. Bake and eat.

TO MAKE MINT COOKIES:
Take 1/2 Andeas Mint and place on top of the baked cookie right out of the oven. Let melt and swirl with toothpick.

Bake 350° for 9 min.

Popcorn Cookies

Submitted by Kathy Tewes, IA

Place 9 cups popped corn in a brown paper bag sprayed with Pam.

Melt in a pan on the stove on low to medium heat. Stir constantly!!

1 stick BUTTER (must be BUTTER, not MARGARINE)
1- 4 1/2 oz. pkg. CINNAMON RED HOTS
1/4 cup CORN SYRUP

Pour over popped corn and shake bag. Place in microwave for 1 1/2 min. on high. Then shake and repeat for 1 1/2 min. more. Shake and bake an additional 60 seconds. Pour out onto waxed paper to cool!! Great Treat! This will harden and be wonderful! This is a favorite with my bunch.

Special Occasion Cookie

Submitted by Glenda Brown, MD

Easy idea for Round Baking Stone
Use either the Chip (without dip dish) or Round Baking Stone
The kids love a "chocolate chip cookie" decorated for their birthday or any celebration you can think of. Have you ever priced them at the stands in the Mall?
Take a roll of Refrigerated Cookie Dough, left out to soften. Preheat oven to 325. Spread onto either the chip dish or round baking stone. Bake for 18-20 minutes or until done. Decorate accordingly. Great idea to help get bookings!

Brownies with Cream Cheese and Strawberry Topping

Submitted by Karen Vanadestine, CT

1 pkg. PILLSBURY "RICH AND MOIST" BROWNIE MIX (9x13 size)
1 can PILLSBURY VANILLA FROSTING
1 tsp VANILLA EXTRACT
2 (8 oz.) pkg. CREAM CHEESE, softened
1 1/2 cans COMSTOCK STRAWBERRY PIE FILLING

1. Spray Chip and Dip with Pam. Mix brownies according to directions. Cook at 350° for 28 minutes. (Undercook, since the chip and dip holds heat. Cool by placing the Chip and Dip on top of a can, so that the air circulates and cools it faster.)
2. Mix the softened cream cheese with the vanilla extract and frosting. Beat with electric mixer until smooth. Place this mixture on top of cooled brownies.
3. Place the pie filling on top of the cream cheese layer. Cover with plastic wrap and chill for about 3 hours. It is best if made the day before you plan to serve it.

Salted Nut Bars

Submitted by Deb Wolf, IA

CRUST:

Mix 1 package dry yellow cake mix with 2/3 cup melted margarine and 1 egg.

Press into a 9x13 pan. Bake @ 350° for 15 minutes.

Remove from oven and cover it with 3 cups miniature marshmallows.

Return pan to oven until marshmallows are soft. Remove from oven and cool.

FILLING:

In a heavy pan mix 2/3 cup white syrup and 2/3 cup margarine and heat until it bubbles all over.

Remove from heat and add: 1 - 12 ounce bag of peanut butter chips, 12 ounces whole or coarsely chopped salted peanuts, 2 teaspoons vanilla, and 2 cups Rice Krispies cereal. Mix well and spread over cooled crust.

Allow to cool slightly before cutting into small squares. Enjoy!!!

"My Aunt Marie's Chocolate Chip Cookies"

Submitted by Kathleen Axson, IN

2 sticks of MARGARINE in mixing bowl (allow to become room temp)
Add:
3/4 cup BROWN SUGAR
1/4 cup WHITE SUGAR
1 teaspoon VANILLA
Beat in 2 eggs until fluffy and add 1 box vanilla pudding mix (instant or cooking type).
Next, add 2 & 1/4 cups All Purpose Gold Medal Flour with 1 teaspoon baking soda blended into it.

Add 1 cup ENGLISH WALNUTS (optional)
Add 1 pkg. (12 oz.) of CHOCOLATE CHIPS

Bake 5-8 minutes on Home & Garden Bakeware Cookie Sheet in preheated 375° degree oven.
These can be shaped into 1 & 1/2 inch balls and frozen on pan in freezer. Then place into a Ziploc bag in freezer to be baked at a later time.

Tollhouse Marble Squares

Submitted by Connie Eck, PA

2 1/4 cup FLOUR
1 cup softened BUTTER (MARGARINE)
3/4 cup SUGAR
1 tsp. VANILLA
1 cup chopped nuts (opt)
1 (12 oz.) bag semisweet CHOCOLATE SHIPS

1 tsp. BAKING SODA
1 tsp. SALT
3/4 cup BROWN SUGAR
2 EGGS

In a small bowl, combine flour, soda and salt. Set aside.

In a mixer bowl, beat butter, sugar, brown sugar and vanilla until creamy. Beat in eggs.

Gradually add in flour mixture. Stir in nuts, if desired. Spread into a 9x13 baker.

Sprinkle on the chocolate chips over the cookie mixture.

Bake for 2 minutes at 375 degree. Remove from oven and swirl the chocolate chips through the cookie dough. Bake approximately 20 minutes. Cool and cut into bars.

Frankie's Chocolaty Peanut Buttery Chip Cookies

Submitted by Rita & Frankie Folena, IL

3/4 cup BUTTER FLAVORED SHORTENING
1 1/4 cups firmly packed LIGHT BROWN SUGAR
2 tablespoons MILK
1 tablespoon of VANILLA
1 EGG
13/4 cups ALL-PURPOSE FLOUR
1 teaspoon of SALT
3/4 teaspoon BAKING SODA
1/4 teaspoon CINNAMON
2 cups semisweet CHOCOLATE SHIPS
1 small bag of PEANUT BUTTER CHIPS (reeves are the best)

*Heat oven to 375 degrees F.
*Combine butter flavored shortening, brown sugar, milk, and vanilla in large bowl. Beat at medium speed of electric mixer until well blended. Beat egg into creamed mixture.
*Combine flour, salt, baking soda and cinnamon. Mix into creamed mixture just until blended. Stir in chocolate chips and peanut butter chips.
Drop rounded tablespoonfuls of dough 3 inches apart on to baking stone. Bake between 10-14 minutes. It really depends on the heat of your oven and the amount of dough used.
As soon as they come out of the oven take them off of the stone and put them on brown paper bags.
This batch will make about 3 dozen gooey cookies.

Class Act Brownies

Submitted by Kathie Van Loon, MI

FANCY BAKING DISH (CHIPPER) OR 9X13 BAKER
1 pkg. (21 oz.) BROWNIE MIX (bake according to instructions)
3/4 cup SEEDLESS RASPBERRY JAM
   (can add fresh raspberries to this if available).
2 8 oz. pkgs. CREAM CHEESE   1/2 cup POWDERED SUGAR
1/4 cup MILK   1 8 oz. COOL WHIP
CHOCOLATE CURLS (optional)

After baking brownies and allowing to cool to room temperature, spread the jam over the brownies. Combine cream cheese and powdered sugar. Mix well. Fold in the Cool Whip. Spread carefully over the jam. Top with chocolate curls (optional) Refrigerate for 1 hour minimum. Cut into wedges or squares to serve. It's almost sinful! Enjoy!

Chip-n-Snowman Dipper

Submitted by Barb Ubienski, OH

It's really easy. You need:
CHIP & DIPPER, DIP BOWL
1 GLASS BOWL or GLASSES smaller than the dip bowl
1 SHOT GLASS
1 pkg. of BROWNIE MIX
1 pkg WHITE FROSTING

Simply take your Chip-N-Dipper and spray everything with "PAM" including the outside of the bowls and shot glass. Mix your brownie mix.

Arrange your dip bowl and med bowl, glass and shot glass to form a snowman shape.

Pour brownie mix into chip plate around the bowls and glasses and bake as instructed.

When it has finished baking, let cool, and remove bowls to reveal the snowman shape.

Fill snowman shape with white frosting and use your imagination to dress the snowman.

Some ideas:
Raisins or mini chocolate chips for eyes and mouth and buttons or cloves, but I like the eatable things better. Toothpicks for the arms. (I took stickers & cut out little gloves and stuck them to the toothpick to form little hands). Licorice or a stick of chewing gum cut in half to make a scarf around his neck and to form a top hat. A carrot sliver for the nose.

(continued)

Or you may use the ready made decorating or drawing tubes available in many colors.

Then take a little of your left over frosting and add a drop or two of food coloring. Mixing color completely.

Then take wax paper & roll it into a cone or funnel shape (just a small opening at one end and larger opening at the other.) Take colored frosting and put into cone fold over the larger opening and roll it down. (It takes only minutes to do and everyone thinks you spent all day in the kitchen preparing & creating just for them!!)

If the different sized cups or bowls are not oven safe, then use the chip bowl and the bottom of the plate. Pour brownie mix in around the bowl only & bake.

When it cools use the other sized cups as cookie cutters and cut the shape out. Then fill and decorate!

This is great easy fun to do with your kids as well.

White Chocolate Chip W/Macadamia

Submitted by Darleen Olszta, MA

(Revised Toll House Chocolate Chip Recipe)
It cooks well on our new rectangular baking stone!
2 1/4 cups ALL PURPOSE FLOUR
1 tsp. BAKING SODA
1 tsp. SALT
1 cup (2 sticks)BUTTER
3/4 cup granulated SUGAR
3/4 cup packed BROWN SUGAR
1 tsp. VANILLA EXTRACT
2 EGGS
1 1/2 cups white CHOCOLATE SHIPS
1 cup MACADAMIA NUTS

Preheat oven to 350°
Combine flour, baking soda, salt in small bowl. Beat butter sugar, brown sugar, and vanilla in our mixing bowl, add eggs one at a time, and beat well after each. Gradually beat in flour mixture, and stir in white choc chips and mac nuts. Drop by rounded tablespoons onto ungreased baking stone.
Bake for 10 minutes or till golden brown. Let stand for approx. 2 minutes then remove to wire racks to cool completely.
These are fast and easy and the kids love them! P.S. Husbands crave them!!

Peanut Butter Carrumba Bars

Submitted by Kim Kennebeck, IL

(Just a few calories here)

CRUST:
1 pkg. YELLOW CAKE MIX (with pudding in the mix)
1/2 cup BUTTER or MARGARINE, melted
1 EGG
1 (6-oz.) pkg. (ten .6 oz. cups) CHOCOLATE-COVERED PEANUT BUTTER CUPS, chopped

FILLING:
1 (1 2.5 oz.) jar (1 cup) CARAMEL ICE CREAM TOPPING
1/4 - 1/3 cup PEANUT BUTTER
(depending how much you love peanut butter)
2 tablespoons CORNSTARCH
1/2-3/4 cup SALTED COCKTAIL PEANUTS
TOPPING:
1 can MILK CHOCOLATE FROSTING SUPREME
2 tbsp MOCHA-FLAVORED INSTANT COFFEE BEVERAGE POWDER
1/2 cup SALTED COCKTAIL PEANUTS, chopped

Heat oven to 350 F. Grease Home & Garden Party's 9x13" pan. In a large bowl, combine all crust ingredients; beat at low speed until well blended. Lightly press in greased pan. Bake at 350 F. for 18 to 22 minutes or until light golden brown.

(continued)

In small saucepan, combine all filling ingredients except peanuts. Cook and stir over low heat until peanut butter is melted. Remove from heat; stir in 1/2-3/4 cup peanuts. Spread evenly over crust. Return crust to oven and bake an additional 5-7 minutes or until almost set. Cool completely.

In small bowl, combine frosting arid beverage powder, mix well. Spread over cooled filling; sprinkle with peanuts. Makes 36 bars.

NUTRITION INFORMATION PER SERVING
1 BAR

Calories	230
Protein	3 g
Carbohydrate	30 g
Dietary Fiber	1 g
FAT	11 g
Polyunsat.	2 g
Saturated	4 g
Cholesterol	14 mg
Sodium	200 mg
Potassium	110 mg

Dietary Exchanges: 1 starch, 1 fruit, 2 fat

Pineapple Squares

Submitted by Joy Blovin, MA

1 pkg dry YELLOW CAKE MIX
1/3 cup (3/4 stick) melted OLEO or BUTTER
1 EGG - slightly beaten
1/2 cup finely chopped WALNUTS

Mix cake mix with walnuts, and add melted oleo and egg and mix till mixture holds together slightly or the size of peas. Place 1/2 mixture in bottom of CHIP & DIP platter, and press firmly. Bake 350° - 15 min - cool slightly.
Meanwhile - Prepare Filling:

1 can (20 oz.) CRUSHED PINEAPPLE WITH JUICE
2 tbsp. CORNSTARCH
3 tsp. SUGAR
1/2 cup cold WATER

Mix cornstarch & sugar till all lumps are removed; add water and stir till all dissolve. Place pineapple into sauce pan and heat on stove till almost boiling. Add cornstarch mixture & cook till thickened, about 2-3 minutes.
Cool slightly. Take Prepared Crust. Spread pineapple mixture over top. Place remaining cake mixture on top. Press down lightly. Bake 350° 25-30 min or until lightly golden - cool, cut into small pie wedges.

7 Layer Cookie

Submitted by Cindy Elliott, OH

1 stick of BUTTER melted in bottom of 9x13 baker
(sprinkle ingredients in order given)
1 cup crushed GRAHAM CRACKERS
1 cup FLAKED COCONUT
1 package 6 oz. BUTTERSCOTCH BITS
1 package 6 oz. CHOCOLATE BITS
dribble 1 can EAGLE BRAND MILK
1 1/2 cups chopped PECANS

Do not stir - bake 350 for 30 minutes. Do not cut until cool.
Or can be split and baked in two Chip & Dip

Jumbo Double Chocolate Cookies

Submitted by Joy Blouin, MA

1 pkg. (21.5) BROWNIE MIX
1/4 cup FLOUR
1/4 cup VEG. OIL

3 tbsp. WATER
2 EGGS
1 cup CHOCOLATE CHIPS

Oven 375° Lightly grease baking stone. Mix brownie mix (dry), flour, oil, water and eggs. Stir in chocolate chips. Drop huge tablespoon amount onto stone. Bake until set - about 15-17 minutes. Let stand 2-3 minutes before removing. Cool completely. Makes about 20-24 large Cookies.

Chocolate No Bake Cookies

Submitted by Brenda Onan, KY

These are cookies that we had in school that all the students were crazy about.

1 large can HERSHEYS SYRUP
1 18 oz. jar of PEANUT BUTTER
1 box DRY POWDERED MILK
1 tablespoon of HONEY GRAHAM CRACKERS

Mix hersheys syrup and peanut butter together. Mix well. Add 1 tablespoon of honey - mix well. Add dry powder milk a little at a time until you can form a log. Then roll the log in graham cracker crumbs, chill and slice.

Frankie's Cupboard Clearing Cookies

Submitted by Rita & Frankie Folena, IL

3/4 cup BUTTERY FLAVORED SHORTENING
1 1/4 cup firmly packed LIGHT BROWN SUGAR
2 tablespoons of MILK
1 tablespoon of pure VANILLA
1 EGG
1 3/4 cups ALL-PURPOSE FLOUR
1 teaspoon SALT
3/4 teaspoon BAKING SODA
1/4 teaspoon CINNAMON
1 1/2 cups RICE KRISPIES
2 kid handfuls of COCONUT (an 8 year old boy size)
2 cups CHOCOLATE CHIPS
1/4 cup chopped WALNUTS

1) Heat oven to 375 degrees F. Place paper bags on counter tops or table.

2) Combine shortening, brown sugar, milk, and vanilla in large bowl. Beat at medium speed until well blended, and then beat egg into cream mixture.

3) Combine flour, salt, baking soda, and cinnamon. Mix into creamed mixture just until blended. Stir in rice krispies, coconut, chocolate chips and walnuts.

4) Drop rounded 1 1/2 tablespoons of dough 3 inches apart onto your pizza stone. Bake for about 13 to 15 minutes for your scrumptious cookies. You may want to cook a little longer or shorter depending on how you like your cookies.

You want to take them off the pizza stone ASAP. Otherwise, they will continue to cook. They cook great on the pizza stone.

"Better Than Oreos"

Submitted by Wendy Peterson, ID

I have actually tested and tried this fabulous recipe. And it is great to use on the round baking stone. It's very simple and quick.

2 packages DEVILS FOOD CAKE MIX (not with pudding) and any flavor
1 1/2 cup CRISCO
4 EGGS
FROSTING OF YOUR CHOICE

Mix all ingredients well. Ball into quarter size shapes, and spread 1-1 1/2 inches apart, enough to spread out. Place on Home and Garden Party baking stone. Bake at 350 degrees for 9 minutes. Let cool and spread on frosting (or not).

The Best Cookies Ever

Submitted by Catherine Alton, CA

3 BOXES YELLOW CAKE MIX
    (whichever brand is on sale-stock up)
EGGS and OIL
    (according to the back of the cake mix box)
1 bag of any type of CHOCOLATE CHIPS -
    (if giving as a gift, then use gourmet chips or M&M chips)

Mix together in large bowl and drop by spoonfuls onto the rectangular baking stone. Bake 10 to 12 minutes until light brown.

(continued)

TEENAGER VERSION:

Use 4 boxes of cake mix and 1 bag of imitation chips. They are going to inhale them anyway, so keep the cost down.

COOKIE PIE VERSION:

Use 2 boxes cake mix and 1 cup chocolate chips and bake in the chip and dip (Pam it first) for 30 to 35 minutes until light brown. You can also use chocolate cake mix with peanut butter chips. However, you can't tell when the cookies are done, so bake one batch of yellow cake mix and one batch of chocolate cake mix at the same time and when the regular cookies are light brown—then the chocolate cookies are also done.

Cranberry Cheesecake Bars

Submitted by Sue Sarbaugh, WI

CRUST:
1 pkg. PUDDING INCLUDED BUTTER RECIPE CAKE MIX
1/2 c. MARGARINE or BUTTER softened
1 EGG
1/4 c chopped PECANS
FILLING:
1- 8 oz. pkg. CREAM CHEESE, softened
1/4 c POWDERED SUGAR
1/2 tsp VANILLA
1 EGG
1- 16 oz. can WHOLE BERRY CRANBERRY SAUCE
1/4 tsp. NUTMEG

In large bowl combine cake mix margarine and 1 egg at low speed until crumbly. Add pecans. Mix well. Press evenly in bottom of CHIP & DIPPER.
Bake at 350° for 10-12 minutes or until crust is set (crust will not be brown).
In small bowl combine cream cheese, powdered sugar, vanilla and 1 egg. Beat until smooth. In another bowl combine cranberry sauce and nutmeg. Blend well and pour cream cheese mixture over partially baked crust. Spoon cranberry sauce lengthwise in 3 rows over cream cheese. Pull knife through cranberry sauce to form swirls. Bake at 350° for 30-40 minutes cool. Yum!

Apple Pie

Submitted by Sue Sarbaugh, WI

I make it in the CHIP & DIPPER
CRUST:
2 cups FLOUR
1 tsp SALT
3/4 cups CRISCO
6-8 tbsp. WATER

Mix flour salt and crisco until blended. Add water until ball forms. Roll out and put in bottom of CHIP & DIPPER (Peel alot of apples to fill).

Make a mound of apples on top of apples. Mix 1 cup sugar and 1 tsp cinnamon and 3 tbsp. flour…Sprinkle over apples. Cut 3 chunks of butter and put on top of apples. If you have dough left over, roll out, cut slits in the dough and set on top of apple mixture. You may have to double the dough recipe. Bake at 410 degrees for 20 minutes and then turn down to 350 degrees for 30 minutes…enjoy!

Candy

Grandma Ray's Million Dollar Fudge

Submitted by Annette DeMay, OH

4 1/2 cups WHITE SUGAR
1 can EVAPORATED (PET) MILK
2 teaspoons BUTTER
DASH SALT

Mix in large pot on stove. Let come to boil. Continue stirring while mixture boils for 7 minutes. Remove from heat.
Add:

2 bars GERMAN CHOCOLATE
2 bags CHOCOLATE CHIP - 12 oz. each
2 cups MARSHMALLOW WHIP CREAM

Mix quickly as fudge sets up fast. Pour fudge into the wonderful 13 inch Home & Garden Party platter. Smooth with spatula. Refrigerate till cool. (I used to take this fudge, by request, to all kinds of outings. I would cut it ahead of time as not to have to take my plain glass baking dish. Now it goes uncut to show off the pretty platter when the fudge is gone which doesn't take long at all!)

Chip and Dip Chocolate Strawberries

Submitted by Leverna L. Garoutte, CA

Rinse and Chill strawberries as well as chip and dip platter.
Arrange strawberries around outside.

In the middle place the melt warmer with a tealight and in the
well (or in the dip bowl placed on top of the well if you desire a
deeper container). Place chocolate chips or candy melts. Chocolate
will be kept melted and warm for dipping,

Chip Dipper
Peanut Butter Fudge

Submitted by Karen Weber, MO

Follow the recipe right down to the 25 large marshmallows and
enjoy!

5 cups SUGAR	3 1/2 cups MILK
2 Tablespoons VANILLA	25 large MARSHMALLOWS

1 8 oz. jar PEANUT BUTTER (any brand)
1 cup slightly crushed BLACK WALNUTS (optional)

Boil sugar and milk until a little dropped into cold water forms a
hard ball (about 1 hour). Add marshmallows and vanilla. Stir until
dissolved. Stir in peanut butter and nuts.

Pour into buttered CHIP & DIPPER before liquid hardens in kettle.
Cool and cut into squares, ENJOY!

Peppermint Popcorn

Submitted by Karen Weber, MO

Pop enough popcorn to fill a large brown grocery sack about 3/4 full.

Use a hammer and gently break one large candy cane into small pieces. You can also crush two or three boxes of the regular canes if you can't fine a large one. I crush mine in sandwich bags.

Sprinkle the candy cane on top of the popcorn. DO NOT STIR!!! Set aside.

Use the following ingredients:

3/4 cup GRANULATED SUGAR
3/4 cups BROWN SUGAR (packed)
1/2 cup LIGHT CORN SYRUP
1/4 teaspoon SALT
1 teaspoon WHITE VINEGAR
1/2 cup WATER

Combine sugars, corn syrup, water, vinegar and the salt in a 2 quart saucepan. Heat to boiling over medium high heat. Stir frequently. Cook stirring constantly until a small amount of mixture dropped into cold water forms a hard ball. (or to 260 degrees on a candy thermometer.)

Reduce heat to low and stir in 1/2 cup butter and 3 or 4 drops of red food coloring. Pour mixture in a thin stream over popcorn in the bag. Use a large container if you don't have a larger paper bag, but a bag is the best. Stir popcorn with a large spoon covering as much of the popcorn as possible. Break bag open and spread out the popcorn and allow to cool for about an hour. (TRY to keep everyone out until it cools if you can!!!) Break apart pieces and put in HOME & GARDEN'S LARGE MIXING BOWL. Serve smaller portions individually in HOME & GARDEN'S CEREAL BOWLS!!! Looks really pretty in the APPLE design!!